THE EASTERN ORTHODOX CHURCH

HUTCHINSON'S UNIVERSITY LIBRARY

CHRISTIAN RELIGION

EDITOR:

THE REV. PROFESSOR E. O. JAMES

M.A., D.LITT., PH.D., D.D., F.S.A.

*Professor of the History and Philosophy of Religion
in the University of London*

THE EASTERN
ORTHODOX CHURCH

by

R. M. FRENCH

1951
HUTCHINSON'S UNIVERSITY LIBRARY
Hutchinson House, London, W.1.

New York   Melbourne   Sydney   Cape Town

*Printed in Great Britain
at the Gainsborough Press, St. Albans,
by Fisher, Knight and Co. Ltd.*

TO
MY WIFE

CONTENTS

PREFACE

NOT only political events in the east of Europe, but also the growing desire for unity among the various bodies of Christians, in the face of a world largely indifferent or hostile, have caused the Orthodox Church to figure a good deal more prominently in the minds of people of the twentieth century than it did in the minds of their fathers and grandfathers.

I have tried to give a picture of the Orthodox Church for the use of the general reader who wishes to know something about Orthodoxy and the significance of the Orthodox Church in Christendom.

It is my hope that the book may be of some service also as a general introduction for students who intend to pursue the study of Orthodoxy further in larger books which deal with various aspects of the subject.

Necessarily much has had to be omitted, but I hope that something approaching due balance and proportion have been preserved in what is left. My debt to works written and edited by Mr. Norman Baynes will be clear. I have an additional reason for thanking him, in that he has been kind enough to read my book before it was sent to the printer and to make some valuable suggestions for its improvement. I am most grateful also to Dr. Dvornik, who kindly read Chapters V and VI, and gave me some criticisms; and to Mr. H. St. L. B. Moss for his help and advice. But I alone am responsible for any faults the book may have.

My obligations to other writers are acknowledged in the appropriate places, and I trust that none have been omitted.

The latter part of Chapter VIII, which deals with Orthodox Church Services, is based upon, and often quotes, what I had already written in *Liturgy and Worship*, published by the S.P.C.K. to whom I express my thanks for permission to use it thus.

My thanks are due also to Miss K. E. Dickson, who patiently spent much time and labour in typing and who made the index.

R.M.F.

Hampstead, 1950.

INTRODUCTION

THE subject of this book is those organized bodies of Christians which formed the original nucleus of Christendom in Apostolic times, together with those Churches which owed their foundation directly to that nucleus and have not since broken their communion with it. That, at least, is a rough and ready description of the Eastern Orthodox Church. It consists of a number of independent and self-governing Churches which together constitute the second largest organized body of Christians in the world. Geographically they lie for the most part at the meeting of East and West, and this has been a dominating fact in shaping their destinies and in forming their distinctive character. East meets West in Russia in the north, and again in the South where Asia juts out westwards to touch Europe on the one hand and Africa on the other.

The Orthodox Church presents a spectacle of the most venerable antiquity and often of an impressive continuity of life which is second to none in Christendom. Its territory embraces the land where Christ himself was born and lived and died. It includes bishoprics in cities of which the names are already familiar words in the New Testament, Jerusalem itself, the Mother of all Churches, and Nazareth; Antioch where "the disciples were first called Christians", and many others. When St. Paul sailed out from Antioch, as many another after him in the history of that great Christian centre, he founded Churches some of which are flourishing centres of Orthodoxy to this day, though from others the glory has long since departed. He wrote letters to the Corinthian Church: the former Archbishop of Corinth, now Archbishop in America, was at one time Dean of the Greek Cathedral in Bayswater. One of the Seven Churches of the Book of Revelation was Thyatira: there is still a Metropolitan of Thyatira, though the

Christian population of the place was wiped out a century ago, and its late Archbishop, Germanos, lived for many years in London.

It is not as simple a matter as might be supposed to enumerate exactly all the independent Churches which are constituent members of the Orthodox Communion. The tumultuous events of the two world wars have left some of them in an uncertain position. It is a general principle of Orthodoxy that an independent nation has an independent Church; it is also an Orthodox principle that such ecclesiastical independence requires the recognition of the parent Church. Thus the various Churches of the Balkans became self-governing after the peoples concerned wrested their political independence from the Turks in the nineteenth century, and in due course their ecclesiastical independence was recognized by the Mother Church of Constantinople. The same parent Church has more recently (1927) granted autocephalous status to the Church of Albania. But political independence takes time to establish securely, it may even prove to be transitory. Moreover, parent Churches may display a very human reluctance to recognize the fact that their daughters have grown up.

There are organized Orthodox Churches in the Baltic States—in Esthonia, Latvia and Finland—as well as in Czechoslovakia, whose autonomy has been recognized by Constantinople. The Church of Georgia too, which was for long absorbed into the Russian Church, has, under the Soviet régime, regained its ancient independence. There is a difference in the degree of independence. An autocephalous Church is entirely independent and self-governing. It appoints its own chief bishop and conducts its relations with other Churches directly. Autonomous Churches are also self-governing and manage their own internal affairs. But the appointment of their chief bishops requires the sanction of the Mother Church, and it is through the Mother Church that their relations with other Churches are carried on.

Up to a point an order of precedence among the autocephalous Churches is recognized. Thus the four ancient patriarchates come first, in this order: Constantinople, Alexandria, Antioch, Jerusalem. Then comes the Church of the Island of Cyprus, after which there is no strict order of dignity. They are enumerated here roughly according to the number of their adherents, Russia, Rumania, Yugoslavia, Greece, Bulgaria, Poland, Georgia, Albania, Sinai. To these must be added the autonomous Churches of Finland, Esthonia, Latvia and Czechoslovakia.

It will be seen that the order of precedence by no means corresponds to relative size. The Russian Church is still, in spite of events since 1917, immensely the largest of them all, while the ancient Patriarchates have flocks numbering at most a hundred thousand or so each, and some much less. But Constantinople, the Ecumenical Patriarchate—shorn as it is of almost all its former splendour and dignity externally—retains its hold upon the reverence of the whole Orthodox Communion as the first of all its sees and the centre of its unity. The smallest of all these Churches is Sinai, which consists of no more than the Monastery on the mountain of that name and contains a score or so of monks.

In the Churches of Alexandria and Jerusalem, the Patriarch himself and the rest of the hierarchy are Greeks, but the enormous majority of their flocks are Arabic speaking, and the relations of these two elements have, in modern times, given rise to some dissensions.[1] The position was similar in the Patriarchate of Antioch, until in 1900 the Arab-speaking Orthodox succeeded in securing the appointment of a Patriarch of their own race and language.

In the Balkan peninsula the Ecumenical Patriarchate and the Church of Greece are, of course, Greek, both racially and linguistically. The Serbs to the north of them are Slav, the Bulgars are a mixed race. Both use forms of Slavonic speech akin to Russian. In the midst of this great tract of Slavdom is embedded the Rumanian Church. The Rumanians claim to be a people of Latin origin and their tongue is derived from Latin. The fact that they are Orthodox by religion provides an interesting contrast to the Poles, who are Slav by race, but prevailingly Roman Catholic in religion.

All these belong to what might be called the home lands

[1] See the Bertram and Young Report (Oxford University Press, 1926 for the Patriarchate of Jerusalem.

of Orthodoxy, they are all places in which the Orthodox Church has been established for many centuries. But adherents of the Orthodox Communion are to be found in groups of varying size and importance in many other parts of the world. Russian imperial expansion under the successors of Peter the Great led them far afield to the north and the east, and again the Russian Revolution scattered them in all directions in the present century. Colonists from the Balkan countries have sought new homes in the New World, and many of them have settled in different parts of the British Empire. Thus the organized Church life of the Orthodox has extended far beyond its homelands and something of this modern expansion of Orthodoxy and its significance will be said in the last chapter of this book.

Everywhere it has borne with it its two names. To the Greeks it is the Orthodox Church, the Church which has received, which guards and teaches the right belief. To the Slavs it is "pravoslavny"—the Church which praises and worships aright. Each name expresses a cherished conviction which belongs to the very core of Orthodoxy. "The Orthodox Church" is its name in English. "The Greek Church" is too narrow, for many, indeed most Orthodox are not Greek. "The Eastern Church" is too wide, for Eastern Christendom includes beside the Orthodox, the Separated Churches of the East.

The latter fall outside the scope of this book which is concerned with the Orthodox Communion only. But for the sake of clearness it may be well to add a few paragraphs here to show who they are and to distinguish them from the Orthodox East, particularly as the interest which attaches to them and their historical significance is out of all proportion to their numbers.

The first group consists of the people commonly called the "Assyrians". Now but a handful of refugees they are the remnants of the once mighty "Church of the East". The Church of Persia, as it then was, asserted its independence in the fifth century, and it has been separated from the Orthodox since the time of the Council of Ephesus, the decrees of which it refused to accept, and thus became, theoretically at any rate, "Nestorian".[1] It lay outside the confines of the Roman Empire and the Persian rulers were by no means averse from this doctrinal cleavage between their Christian subjects and the Churches of the Great Empire across their frontiers. In the seventh century the Arabs destroyed the Persian Empire, but under its Moslem masters the Nestorian Church continued to flourish and sent out its missions all across the Continent, even as far as Pekin and the Malabar Coast of South India.[2]

The whirlwind of Genghis Khan's brief dash into the West about the year 1220 led to some interesting contacts between Europe and the Far East and stimulated missionary activity. But the appalling campaigns of Tamerlane, a century and a half later, wiped out completely the splendour of the Nestorian Church. An island of Christianity (which, however, turned Monophysite in the seventeenth century) remains to this day at Malabar, to bear witness to its missionary activity. The survivors of the Mother Church escaped to the highlands of Kurdistan, where they continued to live under a Patriarch whose office became hereditary by transmission from uncle to nephew. These are the "Assyrians" who fought on the Allied side in the first world war. But the hurricane of world events focused in the ferocity of the Turks who after 1918 again devastated this gallant and much suffering little people. Some of the remnants have settled in Syria; but they are without their Patriarch Mar Shimun, who as a boy was educated in England under the care of the Archbishop of Canterbury, and now lives mainly in America, where a portion of his flock resides.

A similar sort of story belongs to the other group of the Separated Eastern Churches—those known as Monophysites. There is this difference, however, that whereas the Nestorians dwelt outside the Roman Empire, a large section of the Monophysites, though by no means all, lived within it. Thus the strong political element which entered into the religious divisions was, in the case of the Nestorians (and also of those Monophysite Armenians who were dominated by the Persians) part of the rivalry between the Empires of Rome and Persia.

---

[1] See page 27.
[2] For the evidence, see Kidd *The Churches of Eastern Christendom*, London, p. 420.

In the case of the Monophysites of Syria and Egypt it was an expression of nationalism in revolt against Byzantine dominance. The Monophysites consist of the Armenians, the Jacobites (in Syria), the Copts (in Egypt) with their daughter Church, the Abyssinians. To these must be added the Christians of Malabar who, as noted above, renounced their original Nestorianism and became Monophysite three hundred years ago. Christianity reached Armenia as early as the third century, and the building up of the Church there was largely due to the work of St. Gregory the Illuminator, at the beginning of the following century. The Armenian Church rejected the decision of the Council of Chalcedon almost at once and it has remained Monophysite throughout the tragic history of the Armenian people. They have been submerged by the successive floods of Persian, Arab, Mongol and Turkish conquest. They have suffered persecution and massacre, but they have survived to live more happily under the Soviet régime than has been their lot for many centuries.

The Jacobites and the Copts represent the original Christian population of Syria and Egypt respectively. The story is much the same in each case. The attempt to impose the decision of Chalcedon upon these parts of the Empire provoked a violent reaction in which doctrinal differences in the interpretation of the faith served as a vehicle for the expression of racial and political animosity. Breaking away from the "Melchites" ("Imperialists") as they dubbed their opponents, they formed independent Monophysite Churches which have continued to this day, leaving but a numerically insignificant minority of loyal adherents of the Orthodox Patriarchs of Alexandria in the one case and of Antioch in the other.

The Jacobites derive their name from one James (Jacobus) Baradaeus—"the ragged"—a picturesque and vigorous personality who devoted his life to organizing the Syrian Monophysites into an independent and rival Church within the Patriarchate of Antioch[1]. He died in A.D. 577.

But if the specific treatment of these Separated Churches lies outside the scope of this book, they cannot be ignored, for the political and religious problems which led to these, the

[1] See page 39 (Chapter II).

first permanent schisms within the Christian Church, played a vital part in the historical development of the Orthodox Church.

The following pages are an attempt to show in bare outline a picture of Orthodoxy in its historical setting, its characteristic contribution to the life and thought of the Christian Church and its significance for the Orthodox people themselves. In a picture with so wide a scope, only salient features can be depicted. In the early centuries the fortunes of the Orthodox Church were involved in the prolonged and unsuccessful attempt of the Byzantine civil power to hold the disintegrating Empire together. In the long run, and in spite of divisions within itself, it refused to collaborate in holding the East by compromise with heresy, as later it declined to purchase material support from the West by recognition of the Papal claims.

With the loss of Syria and Egypt in the East, the increasing estrangement from the West, and the incorporation of the Slav peoples into the Orthodox world, the axis of Orthodox consciousness veered round from an east-west direction to one which ran north and south, and Orthodoxy stood alone, conscious of itself as the sole guardian of the integrity of the traditional faith of Christendom, proud of its inheritance of Hellenistic culture and all too aware of the splendour of its civilization. The alienation from the Papacy was accentuated by the latter's recognition of a rival emperor in the West, and the sack of Constantinople by the Crusaders in 1204 both revealed how profound the break between East and West had become and set the seal of permanence upon it.

With the fall of the city in 1453 Greek and South-Slav Orthodoxy went underground, yet succeeded in preserving its life and maintaining its identity. In it the peoples, submerged beneath the rule of Islam, found not only consolation but hope also, and inspiration to cherish their national and cultural aspirations. They looked wistfully northwards to the only Orthodox country which was ruled by Christian sovereigns, to Moscow, itself still isolated from the West, but claiming to be the heir of the glory and Orthodoxy of Byzantium.

A mere glance at such a history helps the understanding of

B

much that is characteristic of Orthodoxy. It is small matter for wonder if the Orthodox are in some ways rigid, if they are conservative and inspired by the conviction that the Faith is above all something to be guarded, if their attitude is defensive with perhaps at times a nuance of what some would call an inferiority complex. History has sentenced them to cherish their faith in the face of opposition, not even Russia has been immune in modern times, and to learn to resist the lure of a material well-being to be gained by abandoning it. As a reward they have their profound sense of the reality of the unseen spiritual world, and their developed genius for corporate worship. Their experience of this world has confirmed their belief that the choice of the monk and hermit who renounce it is the highest expression of the Christian life. They look less for justice in this life than for fortitude to bear injustice and for reverence towards those who suffer, and this blends well with the temperamental melancholy of the Slav. In the beauty and truth of the unseen world they find their consolation, and also their strength, for in the resurrection of Christ they see the guarantee that in the end that world of the Spirit will redeem and transfigure not only human life but the whole cosmos.

PART I

CHAPTER I

FROM CONSTANTINE TO CHALCEDON

In the year 330 the commanding, if in some ways enigmatic, figure of Constantine inaugurated his new capital city and thereby switched the stream of world history into new channels. It was the recognition of facts by genius. For the centre of gravity of the Roman Empire had already shifted to the East, and that for many reasons. It was from the East that came the riches which supplied the luxury the Roman patrician demanded and provided the doles and donatives which kept the populace and the army in good temper. Nor was the harbour of Old Rome able to offer shipping facilities to receive them which could begin to compare with Byzantium, where the harbour was one of the finest in the world. It was in the East of the Empire that intellectual life flourished and men's minds came into direct contact with new movements of thought which were agitating the Mediterranean world. The person of the Roman Emperor himself was conceived after a different fashion from that of earlier days. Ceasing to regard himself as a god, he became the vicegerent of God. He was now a monarch after the Oriental pattern, remote, surrounded by the adulation of an obsequious court.

Thus Constantine, left sole master of the Roman world by his victory over Licinius (324), chose Byzantium for his imperial seat, refounding it, marking out its new boundaries and bestowing his own name upon it. But this city which was to become the bulwark of Christendom for a thousand years, was to have many names on the lips of men as time went on. It was New Rome to its founder and such it officially remained. Almost legendary in its fantastic splendour and power it will be the Mickelgard of the wild Northmen. The Russians will look enviously upon it from their own bleak plains and call it Tsargrad. The Turks, to whom it will finally fall, will call it Istamboul.

The city was built on the peninsula between the Golden Horn and the Propontis, which were connected by walls which still survive. Nature seemed to design, and history confirmed for the City so situated, a double rôle. On the one hand it linked the world of the Black Sea with the Mediterranean world, its shipping passed through the Bosporus to Sinope, Trebizond and beyond to bring the produce of Georgia and the Caucasus. Through the Dardanelles its fleets sailed into the Aegean and the Levant. Constantinople was at various times a great maritime power. On the other hand it was destined to be a great continental and military power, for it was the focal point of the great roads which linked Europe and Asia. Two such, coming from the West through the Balkans, converged upon the city, while the great military and commercial route through Asia Minor to Iconium forked thence north and south to reach the Valley of the Euphrates and connect with trade from the Indies. (In 995 the Emperor Basil moved an army from the Bulgarian Front and brought relief to Aleppo in sixteen days.)

Through these communications the many-sided business of the Empire flowed like blood through the veins, and upon their being kept safe and clear the vitality of the Empire depended. Along them passed and repassed its statesmen, soldiers, and merchants, its bishops to meet in councils, its missionaries of the Christian Faith. Constantine had already made clear that he favoured the new religion which no persecution had been able to destroy, and although he postponed baptism until his deathbed, a practice not unknown at the time, he was a Christian believer himself and was in due course canonized in the East. Before he became sole emperor he had proclaimed freedom for the churches in the West, decreed the restitution of their property without compensation to their present possessors, and made generous donations to churches in

Africa and Italy. After the meeting of the two emperors at Milan, Licinius had issued from Nicomedia a similar proclamation of freedom and restitution for the churches in the East. And when Licinius changed his attitude and grew more hostile again towards the Christians, Constantine made use of his own pro-Christian policy in his final attack upon his rival, and having gained his victory he reiterated his proclamation for the benefit of the whole Roman world. Moreover, New Rome, he determined, should be Christian from its inception.

It will be convenient here to review briefly the geographical expansion of Christianity by this time.

The founder of the Christian religion had left His disciples with the injunction: "Go ye into all the world and preach the Gospel to every creature", and the stories and legends about the missionary journeys of the Twelve, however unhistorical they may be in detail, at least suggest that the Apostles were eager to give literal obedience to the command. Certainly the new faith spread rapidly: the persecution in which St. Stephen met his death scattered the rank and file of the believers domiciled in Jerusalem, and wherever they went they were bearers of the new faith: the constant movement of men from place to place in the Mediterranean world about their ordinary affairs carried the Christian religion in all directions apart from any definite missionary plan. Already in New Testament times there were Christians to the west in Rome and to the north in Asia Minor and Greece. From Antioch St. Paul set out on his deliberately missionary journeys, in the course of which he founded Christian Churches in many of the strategic centres of the Eastern Mediterranean.

The destruction of Jerusalem in A.D. 70, and the fact that after Hadrian's edict of 135, which forbade Jews to dwell in the city, the Christian Church there was wholly Gentile, finally settled the vexed question of the relation of the church to the synagogue and made clear that the former threw its doors wide open to all men. By the end of the first century the number of Christian Churches had reached one hundred: and three-quarters of them lay in the East. In the following century the expansion continued, more and more Churches came into being on the coasts of the Aegean Sea. Nor were these any longer mere isolated outposts: in some of the provinces of Asia Minor, Phrygia, Cappadocia and Pontus it may be that the majority of the population was Christian by the year 200.

At the same time the Christian faith moved eastward. It crossed the Euphrates about half-way through the century, towards the end of it it had reached Edessa, while further south missionaries from Palestine and Syria were penetrating into Mesopotamia and Arabia. Such conquests became the starting points for still further expansion to the east and north. The Church of Persia probably owed its origin to missionaries from Edessa. The Armenian Church which was to have so tragic a history came into being about the year 280 when King Teridates accepted baptism, and owed much of its organization to St. Gregory the Illuminator who came from the Cappadocian Caesarea. Northwards again the movement spread to the foothills of the Caucasus where the Georgians received their Christianity early in the fourth century. But little later, away in the extreme south of the then-known world, the Abyssinians were receiving a bishop and priests from Athanasius of Alexandria.

By this time Christianity had captured the imperial throne itself and under Constantine found itself a recognized religion in a despotic State. Not yet the only recognized religion, for if Constantine favoured the Church, he did not forget that as emperor he was Pontifex Maximus, and the duties which that involved. If he tried to hold in check divagations from the norm in Christianity, he also exercised a similar control over paganism.

Not until the latter part of the century did Christianity become the one State religion and definitely replace the old paganism as the religious basis of the imperial power. But the reversal in the fortunes of the Church was startling enough. No doubt the imperial favour led to an influx into the Church of many who were but half converted and imperfectly instructed, but the dominant fact was the complete alteration in outlook involved in the exchange of a position of subjection for one of dominance, of fear of annihilation for the hope of converting the Empire, of defiance of imperial edicts for co-operation with the occupant of the imperial throne.

It is not to cast doubt upon the genuineness of Constantine's conversion to draw attention to his conviction that the prosperity of the State was bound up with the unity of the Church, nor to impugn the religious sincerity of his successors to suggest that the emperors sought in the Church a unifying force among their heterogeneous subjects. The unwieldy bulk of the Roman Empire was already showing signs of disintegration, and the primary task of its ruler was to consolidate it and, if possible, secure its unity. The dealings of the emperors with the Church and their intervention in its internal disputes are to be explained not merely by zeal for abstract truth and theological principles but perhaps primarily by a determination to maintain law and order, to preserve at least the semblance of peace and unity. To this end Constantine, "the man of God", as he styled himself, was prepared to go to considerable lengths in intrusion into the domain of ecclesiastical and spiritual affairs, witness his action in the matter of the Donatist schism:[1] while his successors were prepared to suppress heresy and schism by force if need be, or to endeavour to do so.[2] From this point of view the Church failed the Throne, and we may note two chief respects in which this was made clear.

First, the Church had not yet worked out the intellectual expression of its own faith, and in the process of doing so was itself convulsed by discord and rent by factions.

It was inevitable that the brief expression of faith attributed in the Authorized Version to the Ethiopian eunuch, "I believe that Jesus Christ is the Son of God" should, in course of time, be expanded. As men reflected upon their religious experience as Christians they desired to give to it what intellectual explanation they could. When people sought admission into the Christian Church they had to be told, so far as human words could express it, to what beliefs about God and about Jesus Christ they were committing themselves by joining it. The attacks of pagan writers, philosophers or others, called for a reasoned defence and explanation of what the Church

[1] Though it must be remembered that he acted reluctantly after two attempts to get the dispute settled by ecclesiastics.

[2] Baynes' *Constantine the Great and the Christian Church*. (Proc. of the British Academy, 1929.)

really did teach. In particular, the statement "Jesus is the Son of God" is one which opens up long vistas of discussion directly an answer is sought to such questions as: "In what sense is He both God and man? What is His relation to the eternal Godhead, or does the fact that He is both God and man mean that He is two distinct persons at the same time?"

The process of finding official answers to these and similar questions racked and rent the Christian Church over a long period of time. And it should be noted that the task was undertaken on the whole with reluctance. The Church was not eager to define the subtle distinctions of its belief, but it was driven to make the attempt by the necessity of repudiating what it held to be false and, therefore, dangerous solutions of the problems involved. The Councils met and argued and promulgated their decisions, not because it was thought, so to speak, that it was, in general, a good thing that this should be done, but because it was considered imperative that such and such teaching should be disowned and rejected lest it should be successful in masquerading as orthodox Christian doctrine. A further point may be noted. The bishops who assembled in the Ecumenical Councils conceived themselves not as expounding Christian doctrine *de novo* or setting forth what seemed to them at the moment the best expression of Christian belief. They were concerned to proclaim and safeguard the teaching which they had received, to make as clear a statement as might be of the faith as it had been handed down to them and entrusted to their care.

Both points of view, the reluctance to define, and the sense of custodianship of a faith received and to be transmitted intact, have always been characteristics of the East. And, in fact, the great Councils were overwhelmingly Eastern. They met in the East, and the vast majority of the bishops attending them came from Eastern sees. At the first Council of Nicaea, out of the 318 bishops traditionally said to have been present only three are known to have come from the West. At the first Council of Constantinople there were no Western bishops at all among the 150 who constituted the assembly, nor was the Pope even invited to it. This is not to say, of course, that the Western Church had no share in the task of giving intel-

lectual expression to the traditional faith of Christendom.
On the contrary, it had indeed, and from time to time weighty
pronouncements were issued from Rome, pronouncements
which, at times, turned the scale, e.g., the famous *Tome of
Leo*. But in the main, the work was the achievement of the Greek
mind, and it is this that accounts for the statement that the
formulation of the Creed was the last great achievement of
Greek philosophy.

The first of the Ecumenical Councils met in the year 325
at Nicaea, a town in Asia Minor just across the water from
Constantinople. Its purpose was to settle the Arian dispute.
Arius was a priest of Alexandria who had taken exception to
expressions used by his bishop Alexander in a charge to his
clergy. Alexander insisted upon the Unity of the Holy Trinity
in such strong terms that Arius accused him of being Sabellian,
that is to say of confusing the Son with the Father. Arius
himself was a pupil of the martyr Lucian and thus inherited
the point of view of the School of Antioch. This local dispute
at Alexandria was to develop into a controversy which long
agitated the Christian world and threatened to disrupt it
altogether. The teaching of Arius appealed to many people
because in appearance, at least, it simplified things, and
safeguarded monotheism. It made of Christ a created being,
differing in essence from God, and in theory at any rate
capable of sin.

When the assembled bishops at Nicaea were faced by the
teaching of Arius in plain terms they were in no doubt, and
they tore up his suggested creed. The real difficulty was to
decide what to say instead. The most learned bishop in
Christendom, Eusebius of Caesarea submitted a creed which
he said had been for a long time in use in his own Church.
The creed itself was unobjectionable and all parties might
have signed it, and it was, perhaps, with such a mediating
purpose that it was offered to the Council. But it left the actual
point at issue with Arius undecided, and the Alexandrians led
by St. Athanasius were determined that it should be decided.
They persuaded the bishops to amend this creed in such a
way as definitely to exclude Arianism. This was achieved by
the insertion of the word "*homoousios*" so that the Son was

said to be of the same substance with the Father. No Arian could accept this.

But though the Council of Nicaea settled the wording of the creed, which became the official creed of orthodox Christendom, it was far from settling the Arian controversy, which continued to rage in three-cornered form among Orthodox, Arian and Semi-Arian, and with varying fortunes for many years to come. So far as the East was concerned, it was the saintly character, the strong personality and the vigour of the three Great Cappadocian Fathers, Gregory of Nazianzus, Gregory of Nyssa, and Basil of Caesarea, which finally won Asia Minor and Syria to allegiance to the Creed of Nicaea.

When the Second Ecumenical Council met at Constantinople in 381, it solemnly reaffirmed that Creed. Arianism was thereafter suppressed by force, it lost the palace influence which had often served it well in the past, and was driven from the Empire to take refuge among the Goths and other barbarians.

But the enquiring subtlety of the Oriental mind had already led to the rise of other disputes, and especially to those concerned with the relation of the human and the divine in the Person of Christ. In the course of the Arian controversy it had been established as Orthodox doctrine that Christ was divine, that He was human, that He was one Christ and not two. But the further question arose of how these two natures were combined.

One Apollinarius, Bishop of Laodicea, in the second half of the fourth century, who had acquired some prestige by defending Christianity against the Emperor Julian the Apostate and by championing the faith of Nicaea against the Arians, advanced the theory that in the Person of Christ the divine Logos took the place of the human soul. On this showing Christ was the Word of God inhabiting a human body. From this it followed that He was in no true sense man, and could have no real experience of human weakness and liability to temptation. Thus a flame was kindled which spread into a conflagration of even greater intensity than the Arian Controversy, for it led in the end to a permanent schism in Christendom.

The opposition to Apollinarianism came from Antioch with its traditional insistence upon the true humanity of Christ, and where the tendency, as revealed in such great teachers and scholars as Diodore of Tarsus and Theodore of Mopsuestia, who were shining lights of the School of Antioch, was to emphasize the reality of Christ's human experience, even at the risk of separating the two natures and implying two persons. It was in this tradition that Nestorius was trained, and when he became Patriarch of Constantinople in 428, he headed an attack upon the ascription of the title "Theotókos" (usually translated "Mother of God") to the Blessed Virgin Mary. Mary, he said, was the Mother of Christ's human nature only. Nestorius, though it is open to dispute whether he really held the opinions attributed to him, was condemned at the third Ecumenical Council, which was held at Ephesus in 431. He was banished and disappeared from the scene. But the controversy went on, and another attempted solution of the problem of the Person of Christ was advanced by Eutyches. He was accused of confusing or blending the divine and human natures in Christ.

It was not until the fourth Ecumenical Council, at Chalcedon in 451, that a final statement was reached. The Council was the largest which had yet met, over six hundred bishops being present, though beside the four papal legates only two bishops came from the West. But the Pope's statement of doctrine known as the *Tome of Leo* which was read and received with acclamation, was of great importance in securing the verdict of the Council upon the various heresies involved. This verdict was the famous Chalcedonian Definition which proclaimed that Christ was consubstantial with the Father as touching His Godhead and consubstantial with us as touching His Manhood, and that the two Natures concur in one Person, without confusion, without change, without division, and without separation.

Thus, by the middle of the fifth century, orthodox doctrine on the fundamental subjects of the Trinity and the Incarnation was, so far as verbal expression is concerned, settled. This is the doctrine which the Orthodox Communion still holds, and, moreover, holds in common with the whole of the West.

But the Definition was far from putting an end to religious controversy; the renewed dispute to which it gave rise constituted one of the reasons for the failure of the attempt to hold the Empire together.

A *second* disintegrating factor in the situation was the rivalry among the great sees of Christendom, and it was closely connected with the former.

To go back to the earliest times, the bishops who carried on the work of the first missionaries would naturally take up their residence in the towns. It was there that the bulk of their flock would be, and there too the greater, or, at least, the more concentrated scope for missionary work among their pagan neighbours. From these towns other Christian centres would be formed in places nearby and thus a number of Churches would grow up in dependence upon the one to which they owed their origin, and the bishop of the latter would continue to be regarded as having jurisdiction over the bishops of such daughter Churches. But this was not the only criterion. A second consideration was the antiquity of any particular see. Bishops of places with a relatively long Christian history, especially if they could lay claim to foundation by an apostle, or to some sort of association with any of the Twelve, tended to rise in the hierarchical scale. Later on, and particularly after Diocletian had reorganized the civil administration of the Empire, a third principle comes to the fore. That is, as far as may be, to make the ecclesiastical coincide with the civil territorial divisions and to rank a bishopric roughly in accordance with the position of its seat in the civil administration. This is a principle which has persisted in the East and has had greater influence there than in the West where Apostolic origin was held to be of more importance. Rome makes her claim as having been founded by the chief of the Apostles, Constantinople bases hers upon the fact that she is the city of the Imperial Throne and the "New Rome". It was explicitly stated at a Council of Antioch in 341 that the reason for all this was a practical one. People were accustomed to have recourse to the Metropolitan City for the settlement of their civil affairs. It was, therefore, convenient that the Bishop in the Metropolitan City should have a certain jurisdiction over the other bishops in the same province.

The interaction of these three theories thus established in due course a hierarchy of sees, ruled by simple bishops, above these the metropolitans, and highest of all the patriarchs, though this last title came later in that fixed sense. By the time of the Council of Nicaea (325) we find five episcopal thrones occupying this highest rank in the East. They were Alexandria, Antioch, Ephesus, Heraclea, and Caesarea in Cappadocia. Ephesus was the capital of the civil diocese of Asia, and had its venerable associations with the old age of St. John; Heraclea was the capital of Thrace, and Caesarea of Pontus. These three were, however, destined soon to be eclipsed by the rising power of a new Patriarchate, Constantinople, and their bishops to sink into the status of metropolitans.

It must be recalled that two great centres of Orthodoxy in later times, Constantinople and Jerusalem, were of minor importance at that time. Byzantium, to give Constantinople its earlier name, was a simple bishopric subordinate to the Metropolitan of Heraclea. Jerusalem had not recovered from the disasters of 70 and 135, and was a bishopric in dependence upon the Palestinian Caesarea. It was not to recover a position of any significance until the fifth century, while the story of Constantinople's achievement in becoming the primary see of the Orthodox Communion is one of the major themes of Orthodox history.

On the other hand the splendour of Alexandria must be realized. It was the largest city of the East with a population numbering at one time a million. Into its ample harbour flowed the rich trade of the East. There was the famous lighthouse and the still more famous library of hundreds of thousands of books. It was a city of temples, theatres, colonnades. It had a flourishing colony of Jews—and it was the centre of a brilliant intellectual life, the Museum providing the most distinguished school of Greek learning to which scholars flocked from all directions. At Alexandria Philo and Basilides taught and there too a great Christian school was established and adorned by such names as Clement and above all Origen who was esteemed the greatest genius of his age.

The Bishop of Alexandria was, therefore, the bishop of the first city of the East. The Christian Church there claimed to have been founded by St. Mark and, therefore, enjoyed a rather vague connection with St. Peter himself. The prestige of its catechistical school was enormous and among its bishops were men of vigorous character and outstanding ability, such as St. Athanasius (328–373) and St. Cyril (412–444), champions in their day of Orthodoxy against the heretics.

Before the rise of Constantinople no one disputed the predominant position in the East of the Patriarch of Alexandria, with Egypt always solidly behind him and an immense body of fanatical monks ready to emerge from the desert at his call. To this day he ranks second in the Eastern Orthodox hierarchy.

The third is his brother of Antioch. "Golden" Antioch lay some five hundred miles to the north-east of Alexandria and bid fair to rival it. It had been laid out on the "gridiron" street pattern of Alexandria on the bank of the Orontes about three hundred years before Christ. It also was the focus of converging trade routes and became wealthy and populous. But it was thirty miles inland from its port of Seleucia, it was liable to earthquakes and it was exposed to the attacks of the Persians. As a Christian bishopric, however, Antioch was secure in the third place after Rome and Alexandria. Like the former it claimed St. Peter for its first bishop. However that may be, no one could deny the apostolic origin of the Church from which St. Paul set out on his missionary journeys. The third Bishop of Antioch was the renowned Ignatius, who wrote his celebrated letters on his journey to Rome and martyrdom in the year 107. The Emperor Constantine favoured the city and built a splendid church there.

Antioch also had its school of Christian theology which developed a distinctive tradition of its own and she too, like Alexandria, had daughter Churches even beyond the limits of the Empire. As Alexandria sent out its bishops to the Ethiopians in the south, so Antioch reached out to the east beyond the Euphrates and founded a Church whose centre was at Edessa. From Antioch also the Church of Georgia was founded. In the heyday of his glory the jurisdiction of the Bishop of Antioch was widespread indeed. But it had not the homogeneity and solidity of the Alexandrine Patriarchate. The island Church of Cyprus, owing to the prestige it derived from its foundation by St. Barnabas, persuaded the Council of Ephesus in 431 to recognize its independence of Antioch. Twenty years later the Council of Chalcedon separated Palestine and Arabia from Antioch by the creation of the new Patriarchate of Jerusalem. Political troubles severed the connection of Antioch with many Christian communities to the east, and in 538 the Persians sacked Antioch itself and completed the ruin which a severe earthquake had begun some years earlier. No fewer than thirty ecclesiastical synods of varying importance were held at Antioch from the year 264 onwards.

At the beginning of the Christian era Byzantium was a small provincial town of no particular importance and there is no record of the foundation of the Christian Church there. It was not until centuries later that someone brought to birth the legend of its foundation by St. Andrew, and when a bishop of Byzantium emerges in history he is simply a local bishop under the jurisdiction of the Metropolitan of Heraclea. But in the year 330 Byzantium was transformed and refounded by the Emperor Constantine who made it his new capital and gave it his name. The Bishop of Byzantium was now Bishop of Constantinople, of New Rome, the city of the Imperial Throne. It was hardly likely that he would remain a mere bishop under the jurisdiction of the neighbouring town. Nor did he. He was, so to speak, the Emperor's own bishop and he could rely upon his imperial master's support in seeking the aggrandizement of his see.

Deliberate policy worked hand in hand with a widespread recognition of the fitness of things. The Fathers assembled at Constantinople for the second Ecumenical Council in 381 accorded the first place of honour in the Christian Orient to Constantinople, which is to rank next after Rome "because it is the New Rome". Thus the Bishop of Constantinople not only threw off the jurisdiction of Heraclea, but attained the summit in a single bound, in theory at any rate. But it is to be noted that although Rome recognized this Council as Ecumenical and accepted its dogmatic decrees, she protested against this particular canon, the third, and it was some eight hundred years before she consented to acknowledge the position it gave to Constantinople. Whatever the Fathers of 381 intended to imply by the position they conferred upon Constantinople, the latter was not slow to interpret it in terms of jurisdiction, trenching upon what others considered the rights of the great sees of Asia Minor, and even of Antioch.

But the real struggle was with Alexandria which viewed with much uneasiness the growing power of its rival on the Bosporus. Alexandria was strong as the champion of the Orthodox Faith against heresy and for long it kept the upper hand. John Chrysostom was no heretic, but Alexandria succeeded in bringing about his deposition and exile when Chrysostom's stern sermons on morals made him unpopular with the Court. The trial of strength came to another crisis in the matter of Nestorius and his teaching. Nestorius was Patriarch of Constantinople and was accused of dividing the personality of Christ in his anxiety, true to his training in the school of Antioch, to safeguard the real humanity of Jesus. Again Alexandria was victorious and its Patriarch Cyril secured the condemnation of Nestorius at the third Ecumenical Council, which was held at Ephesus in 431.

The all-powerful Egyptian patriarch was to achieve one more triumph before he fell. In 449 at what was afterwards known as the "Robber Council" of Ephesus, Dioscorus of Alexandria led this disreputable assembly in its condemnation of Flavian, Patriarch of Constantinople. The latter was the outstanding opponent of Eutyches the monk who in his attacks upon Nestorius was held to have gone to the opposite extreme and taught that Christ had not only one single personality, but a single nature also. Dioscorus had his own nominee appointed to the Throne of Constantinople, as Flavian's successor. But the supremacy of Alexandria was coming to an abrupt end. It had itself fallen into heresy—the world was tired of its dictatorial attitude, it lost its influence at Court after the death of the Emperor Theodosius II. Only two years after the Robber Council, the fourth Ecumenical Council met at Chalcedon. The teaching of the Monophysites—that Christ had only one nature—was condemned and Dioscorus, inflexible and domineering to the last, went into exile. That meant the end of the dominant position of Alexandria and the triumph of Constantinople in the long drawn-out struggle fought in the field of theology.

The controversy which raged around the alleged teaching of Nestorius and his opponent Eutyches brought about what even Arianism for all its temporary triumphs had failed to do, it made a lasting breach in the unity of Christendom. The mass of the Christian population of Egypt and Syria nominally embraced the doctrine of the Monophysites and refused to accept the Council of Chalcedon, with its definition of Two Natures in the One Person of Christ. They broke away from the unity of Christendom to become the Coptic Church in Egypt and the Jacobite Church in Syria, leaving the Patriarchates of Alexandria, Antioch and Jerusalem as Greek-speaking islands of Orthodoxy, which, with the remnants of their flocks, still remained in communion with Constantinople. From now onwards Constantinople was to remain indisputably supreme in Eastern Christendom.

CHAPTER II

LOSS OF THE EAST

HISTORIANS have noted that whereas Old Rome was geographically well situated to be the capital of a Mediterranean power the same was not true of New Rome on the Bosporus. Geographically, the natural territory of an Empire of which the centre was in Constantinople would include the Balkan peninsula, with the basin of the lower Danube, the littorals of the Black Sea and the Aegean, and Asia Minor, extending possibly to the Caucasus and the Upper Euphrates, and the most brilliant periods of the Empire were those in which the actual territory beneath its sway more or less corresponded to these geographical limits.

But the theory of Rome as a world power was transported from the Tiber to the Bosporus with other conceptions and the apparatus of government. It met too with the sanction and support of religion.

The Church also regarded the Empire as both universal and eternal. The occupant of the throne, whether he reached that position by succeeding his father, or by staging a successful *coup d'etat*, provided his position was confirmed by the acclamation of senate, army and people, was the vicegerent of God. In course of time, it is not known exactly when, this was symbolized in a ceremony added to the coronation rite in which the Patriarch of Constantinople anointed the new ruler with the sacred oil. Whatever steps may have brought him to the throne, once seated upon it the Emperor was the elect of God and there was a religious aspect of his office as well as a secular. As the vicegerent of Christ upon earth, he claims the whole world as the sphere of his dominion whatever appearance to the contrary actual circumstances may shew, *à fortiori*, therefore, should he hold beneath his sway all that Rome ever held.

With this ecclesiastical support to sanction and invigorate their secular pretensions the Byzantine Emperors were committed to the superhuman task of endeavouring to hold, or to recover piecemeal, as the case might be, the whole vast extent of the Roman Empire; to secure it against dismemberment by barbarian attacks from without and against disintegration from disruptive forces within.

Egypt had never been fully absorbed into the life of the Empire, nor was it more so when it was dominated by a series of masterful Patriarchs of Alexandria who wielded more actual power over its turbulent populace than the representatives of the civil government could make effective. Syria too was not only exposed to constant attack from the east and south but was continually at odds with Constantinople about matters both secular and religious. Justinian, that striking figure who combined the ascetic and the student with the vigorous man of action of an immense capacity for work, did indeed at vast expenditure of effort and treasure recover Italy and north-west Africa from the Barbarians. But they were never again completely restored to the unity of the Empire. Like Egypt and Syria they became outlying provinces almost like colonies which readily became a prey to new invaders, who found within them elements which made their task of conquest easier.

In course of time both East (Syria and Egypt) and West were lost. In Syria and Egypt separatist tendencies in the political sphere were combined with continued controversy in ecclesiastical matters. The Council of Chalcedon, for all its unanimity, was far from bringing peace to the Church. It stated the problem rather than solved it. Its assembled bishops may have cried: "We all say the same thing", but the thing they said did not cease to be the matter of further dispute in the Church at large. True the Council had definitely disposed of the heresy of Eutyches. But there were many ready to enquire doubtfully whether in accepting the *Tome of Leo*, it had done sufficient justice to the language of Cyril of Alexandria, which was widely accepted in the East as theologically authoritative. It was noted that though some of his letters were read to the Council, the most crucial, the third letter to Nestorius, which contained the anathemas, was passed over in silence. Moreover the Council had condemned Dioscorus. True this had not been on doctrinal grounds, but might not his condemnation be taken to mean that the Council was not wholehearted in its adherence to Cyrillian doctrine? In any case Dioscorus, Bishop of Alexandria, represented Egyptian national feeling. He had been deposed, and Egypt did not like it.

The hatred which the Egyptian Monophysites felt for the Council of Chalcedon was not based entirely on dogmatic grounds. In its famous 28th Canon the Council confirmed and even emphasized the Canon of the Constantinopolitan Council of 381 which assigned the second place after Rome in the order of precedence to the throne of Constantinople. The undisputed authority so long enjoyed by the Patriarch of Alexandria, his riches and his dignity, did not allow the Egyptians to forget that that second place had once belonged to their own patriarch, and that so it had been recognized at Nicaea.[1]

Trouble broke out almost at once both in Syria and in Egypt, in spite of an imperial rescript imposing the decisions of Chalcedon and forbidding further discussion. To the accompaniment of riots, arson and bloodshed the Orthodox bishops were driven from their sees by hordes of infuriated monks, and regular troops had to be employed to restore some semblance of order.

For many years the story is confused and obscure. Bishops, both Orthodox and Monophysite, are removed from their thrones and reinstated, then expelled and reinstated again. Disorder and violence, at times of a most brutal kind, supplement arguments to sway men's minds and dispose of their fortunes. Definite leaders of Monophysitism emerge into the foreground, Timothy the Cat at Alexandria, Peter the Fuller at Antioch, Peter Mongus, whose vivid careers cannot be followed here.

The emperors made energetic and repeated attempts to

---

[1] At Ephesus in 449, the Latrocinium, Dioscorus of Alexandria called himself "Ecumenical Patriarch", the first recorded use of the title.

reconcile the Monophysites and to restore peace to the Church. Basiliscus put out his *Encyclical* which affirmed the doctrine of Cyril and condemned the Council of Chalcedon. The bishops were all required to sign this *Encyclical* and most of them did. But Acacius the Ecumenical Patriarch steadily resisted it. In the year 482 the Emperor Zeno issued his *Henoticon* which, while emphatically affirming the faith of Nicaea and Constantinople (381), studiously avoided saying anything definite on the points about which people were quarrelling so violently at the time. The *Henoticon* was not expressly heretical, but its allusion to Chalcedon was not exactly happy: the faith of the 318 Fathers (Nicaea) is the one and only faith, whoever thinks otherwise, now or at any time, "at Chalcedon or at any other Council" is anathematized.

Acacius accepted, perhaps indeed inspired, the *Henoticon*. But such attempts to secure peace by compromise did not really satisfy anyone, even though they were accepted in theory by the Eastern bishops. What is more, there was a heavy price to pay for them. It meant discord with Rome. Rome stood for the Chalcedonian Faith and the *Tome of Leo* and would admit no tampering with it. It was indeed an impossible situation. There were many forms of Monophysitism, some more extreme than others; it was entangled with separatist ambitions, especially in Egypt. The Emperors' well-meant efforts to conciliate by compromise, without really achieving their purpose in the East provoked reaction in the West and brought the Pope into the field. Matters came to a head in 484 when Pope Felix III excommunicated Acacius, and some were found with the necessary skill and hardihood to pin (at the cost of their lives) the act of deposition to the Patriarch's vestments while he was celebrating the Liturgy.

This schism between Constantinople and Rome was to last till 518. But by that time a reaction in favour of Orthodoxy had taken place in the East.

The populace of Constantinople insisted upon their Patriarch's acceptance of Chalcedon at a ceremony in honour of that Council in the Church of the Holy Wisdom. The Emperor Justin and the Patriarch wrote to the Pope inviting reconciliation. The Pope Hormisdas responded favourably but sent his legates with instructions to insist upon the removal from the diptychs of the names of Acacius, Zeno and others who had supported the *Henoticon*. This was not an insuperable difficulty. Already the rising tide of Orthodoxy in the East had reinstated many Orthodox bishops who had been imprisoned or exiled. Egypt, it is true, remained unmoved by the imperial order to recognize Chalcedon, and the Emperor Justin found it politic to allow the election of a Monophysite Patriarch. But in Syria even Severus, the outstanding champion of Monophysitism at this time and one of the most learned men of his day, was obliged to abandon his patriarchal see of Antioch and yield to an Orthodox bishop while he betook himself to Egypt.

Justinian, who ascended the Imperial throne in 527, threw all his great abilities and immense energy into a two-fold task, the recovery and consolidation of the whole ancient inheritance of the Caesars, and the establishment of peace and unity within the Church. The recovery was to be accomplished by military conquest, the consolidation by law, of which his will was the divinely appointed source.

It was a grandiose and in many respects a noble enterprise, but the attempt to achieve it exhausted the Empire, the resources of which were unequal to the task. And so far as the Church was concerned the imperial counsels were divided. The remarkable and picturesque Theodora, Justinian's wife, to whom he was much attached, was a woman of great ability and wielded as Empress almost as much power as the Emperor himself. And she was decidedly Monophysite in her sympathies. While Justinian was issuing edicts against the dissidents, Theodora was openly protecting Monophysites even in Constantinople itself. The Emperor sought the establishment of Orthodoxy and union with Rome, but the eyes of the Empress were fixed upon the East. To her the rich lands of Asia, Syria and Egypt were the Empire. Unlike her husband, she was not a theologian, and she was convinced that these Eastern provinces must, Pope or no Pope, be reconciled by wise concessions. There are those who think that from the political point of view she sensed the future more clearly than Justinian. The Emperor himself did not regard Monophysitism, especially of the more reputable type represented by Severus, as on the

same level as other heresies. Renewed attempts to conciliate
the Monophysites met, however, with no more success than
had attended similar efforts in the past. And meanwhile, one
Jacob Baradeus, a monk who had enjoyed the protection of
Theodora, being made bishop, set himself to tour the East
with a view to re-establish and secure the permanence of the
Monophysite hierarchy: and this indeed he did.

In due course Justinian was persuaded to take up the question of the Three Chapters, and he issued an edict in which
on his own authority he condemned them.

The Three Chapters were writings of Theodore of Mopsuestia, Theodoret and Ibas, Bishop of Edessa. All belonged to
the School of Antioch in their theology, and Theodore had
been the teacher and Theodoret the fellow-pupil of Nestorius.
All three had been dead for nearly a century, but the two latter
prelates had been condemned on Dioscorus's charge of
Nestorianism at the Latrocinium of Ephesus, and subsequently
restored at Chalcedon. The question of their condemnation,
or rather recondemnation, played much the same part under
Justinian that the *Henoticon* had played under Zeno—that is
to say it was offered as a bait to catch the Monophysites and
restore unity in the East; and without achieving any permanent
result in that direction, it provoked hostile reaction from
Rome and the West.

In this case, however, the Pope, Vigilius, hesitated in his
pronouncement so long that the Emperor lost patience and
had him kidnapped and brought to Constantinople. There he
was induced to issue the *Judicatum*—condemning the three
writers. The whole of the West protested so violently that the
Pope obtained the Emperor's permission to withdraw his
Judicatum and it was decided to refer the matter to a Council.
This was the Fifth Ecumenical Council summoned in 553.
Only six Western bishops attended, all from Africa. The Pope
refused to take any part in the proceedings, and after considerable delay produced his own decision in a document called
the *Constitution*. While condemning sixty passages from
Theodore of Mopsuestia, he refused to condemn Theodore
himself on the ground that it was not customary to condemn
the dead. Neither would he condemn Theodoret and Ibas,

since Chalcedon had declared them free from heresy. Meanwhile the Council continued its proceedings and in accordance with the Emperor's will it erased Vigilius's name from the diptychs and condemned the Three Chapters. In the end the unfortunate Pope, who had been scandalously treated by Justinian and whose liberty and even life were often in danger, accepted the decision of the Council, but it was long before the West as a whole did the same.

One more great effort to reach agreement with the Monophysites must be noted, and that was associated with the name of the Emperor Heraclius (610 to 641) and with the circumstances of the Persian War. Heraclius's accession to the throne was the result of a revolution which overthrew his predecessor, Phocas, and it occurred at a crisis in which the fortunes of Byzantium were at a very low ebb. The Persian armies had captured the great frontier fortress of Dara already in 604 and were sweeping west and south. In the nature of the case it was the provinces of the Empire in which Monophysitism was predominant which bore the brunt of the invasion. The Persian advance was rapid. Syria was overrun, Antioch fell, Jerusalem was captured in 614, Constantine's Church of the Holy Sepulchre was burnt and the relic of the True Cross despatched as a trophy to the Persian King. The following year Persian raiding parties were crossing Asia Minor without hindrance. In 617 Alexandria fell and all Egypt was occupied. The news of the capture of the True Cross was received in Byzantium with utter consternation. But all this was not the full measure of disaster. The Avars and the Slavs were at the same time invading the Balkan peninsula, settling in the open country and besieging the cities while the populace fled for refuge to the coasts. The Barbarians even pillaged the suburbs of Constantinople. Added to this the city was ravaged by epidemics, and there was no money in the treasury.

It is against such a background that the greatness of Heraclius stands out. He was a man of great strength of character and of indomitable courage. And he was one of the greatest strategists that the Byzantine Empire produced.

His plan was to placate the Avars and secure some sort of peace on that front, however precarious, while he set

methodically to work on a programme of economic internal
recovery and on the preparation of a counter-blow against
Persia. In all this he had the assistance of a Patriarch who was
worthy of him, Sergius of Constantinople, who placed the
treasures of the Church at the Emperor's disposal.

In twelve years' time he was ready and launched his
counterblow. It took the form of an attack upon Persia itself.
Nor did he abandon his plan when the Persian King succeeded
in persuading the perfidious Avars to attack Constantinople,
and the city was besieged by the joint forces of Barbarians and
Persians in 626. This was one of the great moments in Byzantine story, when the city stood out clearly in its historic rôle as
a rampart which prevented the Barbarians of the North from
joining with invaders from the East. The Patriarch Sergius
was the soul of the defence and employed all his eloquence to
maintain the courage of the Byzantines, and all the apparatus
of religion to stimulate their faith and instil terror into their
enemies. Whether the Akathist hymn was composed by
Sergius at this time or whether it belongs to a later period,
certain it is that the Byzantines attributed their deliverance to
the intervention of Our Lady, and instituted a yearly festival
in thankful commemoration of the occasion.

By 628 Heraclius was completely victorious and Persia
was to trouble the Roman Empire no more. Two years later
the Emperor entered Jerusalem in triumph and brought back
with him the True Cross. From the first the religious aspect
of the war had been prominent and has given Heraclius the
title of the First Crusader.

The religious question was never far from his mind. As
so many of his predecessors he saw the political urgency of an
ecclesiastical settlement, and like them he pursued the will o'
the wisp of reconciling the Monophysites. The urgency was
even more apparent now. His predecessor Phocas had exas-
perated the Monophysites by his persecution of them. The
Persian King when he overran the Orient intended to remain
there, and indeed did remain in Syria for eighteen years and
in Egypt for eleven. Chosroes had Christians in his own
country, two of his wives belonged to that religion, and bishops,
both Nestorian and Monophysite, came in the train of his

armies. Everywhere the Orthodox bishops in the invaded provinces were expelled, for Chosroes, though on the whole well-disposed to the Christians, naturally favoured the Monophysite form of their faith, the Orthodox form being the official religion of the Empire he was fighting. Thus, when the war ended, the Monophysites had been living for years under another political allegiance and without being harassed because of their religious convictions. But Heraclius did not wait for the end of the war. He had from the beginning faced the question of religious unity as part of his plans for imperial reconstruction. He had put forth an edict about the Faith which while Orthodox itself revealed in its use of Cyrillian phraseology a desire to reconcile the Monophysites; and it was with imperial sanction that the Copts and Syrian Jacobites had united about 616.

But it was just at that time that the Patriarch Sergius thought he had solved the perennial problem. He suggested a formula which recognized a single "energy" in Christ, behind the two natures and operating through each. Heraclius took up the idea and became convinced that this was really the means for reconciling the dissidents to Orthodoxy. In the midst of his military operations against Persia he found time to urge it upon various Monophysite prelates and he met with striking success. In 633 even Egypt was won over and accepted the new doctrine of the single "energy". Thus Sergius in writing to the Pope to secure his adherence, frankly laid stress upon the happy results in achieving peace and securing the acceptance of Chalcedon which had attended the formula, rather than argued in its theological defence. Pope Honorius agreed, but himself used and recommended the phrase "a single will". Both Pope and Patriarch agreed that once union was reached it would be prudent to drop the discussion of the matter in future and avoid the phrases, "single energy" and "double energy".

All seemed well; but everyone had reckoned without one Sophronius, who had been opposing in Egypt the propagation of the new formula by Cyrus, Patriarch of Alexandria. The weight of his opposition was greatly increased by his elevation to the Patriarchal Throne of Jerusalem at the end of the year

633. On that occasion he issued a synodical letter in which he vigorously asserted the existence of two "energies" in Christ, and argued that the acceptance of a single "energy" really amounted to Monophysitism.

Thus, all was in dispute again, and it became clear that the successes of "monergism" had been more apparent than real. And the Pope's new formula, "one will", could be accepted in different senses, or rather its stress could be applied in different directions. To the Pope it emphasized the unity of Christ's Person, to the Monophysites it implied their own doctrine, that He had but one Nature.

Shortly before his death in 638, the Patriarch Sergius published, in the name of the Emperor, the *Ekthesis*. This celebrated document was an exposition of the Faith of Chalcedon in regard to the Trinity and the Incarnation, which went on to prohibit the phrases "one energy" and "two energies" and affirmed that Christ had a single will. The *Ekthesis* roused a storm of protest both in East and West, and the controversy continued for long after the original protagonists had died. Honorius's two immediate successors (John IV and Theodore) both pronounced against it; the monk Maximus led the opposition in Africa. The Emperor Constantine II issued his *Typos* in which he simply forbade discussion of the matter. But Pope Martin I called a Council at the Lateran and condemned both the *Ekthesis* and the *Typos* more uncompromisingly than ever. Both he and Maximus paid for their boldness, and each in due course died from the effect of the treatment they received. The dispute dragged on and both sides became heartily tired of it. It was not definitely settled until the Sixth Ecumenical Council was called to deal with it in 680. The Council finally condemned monergism and monotheletism and anathematized the principal exponents of the heresy. The names included Sergius of Constantinople and his two successors Pyrrhus and Paul, Pope Honorius, Cyrus of Alexandria and others.

Thus the last attempt to reconcile the dissidents failed as the others had failed. The pattern is familiar. Anxious to strengthen and consolidate the Empire by securing religious unity the imperial authority puts forward proposals which amount to compromise. The proposed formula is backed first by argument and then by force. But concessions which seemed to the Monophysites inadequate, appeared to the West to be unwarrantably great. And the result was no more than interminable dispute. By the time of the Sixth Ecumenical Council the political situation which faced Heraclius and Sergius when they put forward their solution of the "one energy", had passed away. Even if monergism had been successful in reconciling the dissidents, it would have come too late, so far as saving the Empire from dismemberment was concerned.

The Hegira, the Flight of Mahomet from Mecca, took place in 622, the year of Heraclius's counter-offensive against Persia. Ten years later the Prophet died, having returned in triumph to Mecca and imposed his authority and religion upon the Arab tribes. And in 634 the movement of those tribes began.

The hosts of Islam were hardy warriors to whom the war of conquest was a religious act, but the exhausted and disordered state of both the Persian and the Byzantine Empires, the incapacity of the Byzantine generals, the religious strife which divided the Christians, and the hostility of the Jews, who were ready to help the Arabs as they had helped the Persians, all this made the Orient an easy prey. And Heraclius was now a sick man.

The Arabs crossed the Byzantine frontiers in 634, and in three years Syria was conquered. The True Cross was removed for safey to Constantinople from Jerusalem which fell in 637. The flood of conquest spread to Roman Mesopotamia, and at the same time other Arab armies conquered Persia. Then came the turn of Egypt. Alexandria capitulated in 641 and the Arabs pushed on to Tripoli and the West. The speed of the Islamic conquests may be realized from the fact that the battle of Poitiers was fought just one hundred years after the death of Mahomet.

CHAPTER III

ESTRANGEMENT FROM THE WEST

IN spite of the brilliant campaign of Heraclius against the Persians, the seventh century was a period of gloom and decadence. It was also a century of developing changes which made it a critical era in Byzantine History. Spain had been lost two centuries earlier, Africa, so recently recovered from the Vandals, was in imminent danger from the westward progress of Islam. Large tracts of north Italy had been lost to the Lombards. The definite loss of Syria, and still more of Egypt, was an immense impoverishment of the Empire, and with the control of Egypt went the imperial dream of re-establishing the ancient realm of the Caesars. The battleground against Islam was in Asia Minor, or what was still more serious, on the sea; for the seventh century saw the inauguration of an Arab navy.

The Slavs were pressing southwards into the Balkan peninsula and towards the end of the century a new people made their appearance from the north, to cross the Danube and become a recurrent menace to Constantinople for three centuries. These were the Bulgars, a Turanian people who subdued the West Slavs and formed them into a kingdom while adopting their language and culture and giving them their own name in return.

Thus the Empire's lines of communication were in peril. The great northern road round the head of the Adriatic which would bring a traveller to Lyons, for instance, in five weeks' journey from the Eastern Capital, and the southern road which went across the peninsula through Thessalonika to the coast town of Dyrrachium from which Rome could be reached in a week, both so vulnerable since the Barbarian invasion

45

began, were definitely cut. The sea route alone remained, lengthy and hazardous.

The Mediterranean had in the past held the Roman Empire together. Even when there were two rulers, one in the East and one in the West, it remained one empire and it was largely the sea which kept it so. Germanic tribes broke through the land frontiers and reached the sea. When the Vandals crossed into Africa, they administered a severe shock to imperial sea power. But Islam was a different matter, with its uncompromising desert Faith and its contemptuous aloofness from the people it conquered. When Islam established itself along the south-eastern and southern coasts and became a Mediterranean power, the great sea highway was deserted and the sea, from being a unifying element, was converted into a barrier between Christianity and Islam. Ships from Byzantium to Italy must hug the coast. Travel which had made the influence of Eastern art and culture felt as far west as Gaul and Britain and made possible the appearance of ornament from Coptic Egypt in the manuscripts of Ireland, was still further restricted.

But the invasions of Barbarian and of Arab alike were but accelerating a process which was inevitable in the nature of things and had been going on for a long while. When Diocletian decided to share the government of the Roman world with a co-adjutor he recognized the fact by establishing the division of authority upon a geographical basis. Thereafter it was only for short periods that the Empire was governed by a single ruler. As time went on, it became increasingly clear that, in this restricted application also, "East is East and West is West" and common misfortunes from without did but emphasize antagonisms, misunderstandings and ecclesiastical disputes within.

The Empire in the East increasingly disclosed its true Hellenistic foundation. Even before the time of Constantine the influence of Oriental ideas about monarchy, court ceremonial and the administrative hierarchy had made themselves felt. Although they had to make headway against other conceptions of Empire they gradually prevailed, especially as the prospect of restoring the territorial integrity of the old Empire receded further and further. After Heraclius crushed he Persian Empire he took himself officially the title *Basileus*, by which the Persian monarch had been known; and "Basileus" the Byzantine sovereigns remained until the end.

Justinian, himself a native of a Latin-speaking district, had to face the problem of language and found himself obliged to issue his *Novels* in Greek, and under his successors Latin disappeared in official documents. The Byzantines continued to call themselves "Romans", but they wrote the word in Greek and Greek was their tongue. Thus, difference of language was added to the difficulties which Rome and Constantinople experienced in trying to understand each other. Letters between the Pope and Eastern bishops had to be translated and translations were, at times, liable through inadvertence, ignorance or perhaps even falsifications, to be inexact. Gregory the Great, consecrated in 590, did not understand Greek, although he had spent some years in Constantinople. A century earlier, such a scholar as St. Augustine of Hippo only mastered Greek towards the end of his life. Even that prodigy of learning, Photius of Constantinople, whom we shall meet later, did not know Latin, and at the time of the final schism in 1054, when Peter of Antioch received a letter from the Pope, he had to send it to Constantinople to be translated.

The Byzantines regarded themselves as the Romans *par excellence*. New Rome in its wealth and culture, its power and its prestige, was the object of their pride; the traditions and glory associated with the name of Rome, were on the Bosporus. Old Rome on the Tiber had relapsed into barbarism in their eyes and they tended to neglect and despise it. "The West" conjured up thoughts of Ravenna or Milan rather than of Rome. The Emperor Zeno shewed little compunction in deliberately diverting Theodoric and his Goths into Italy in 488.

The Barbarians had, indeed, captured Rome at the beginning of the fifth century, and although their occupation of it did not last, the blow was a shattering one to the prestige of the old imperial capital. By the end of that century the Empire in the West was dead. The last legitimate Western Emperor was assassinated in exile in 480. Thereafter, except for

Justinian's temporary restoration, there was only the rule of
Barbarian kings standing in various relations to the Emperor
at Byzantium.

It was against this background of confusion and political
collapse in the West that the rivalry of the Great Sees of
Christendom, which we have noticed, was working itself out,
and Rome was insisting upon her position as the premier
episcopal throne. Leo I protested vigorously against the
celebrated 28th Canon of Chalcedon, which renewed and
stressed the assignment of the second place to Constantinople,
which had been decided at the second Ecumenical Council
(381). It was long before Rome accepted it. But Constantinople
held to its position. The fact that the great heresies (apart
from Pelagianism) arose in the East strengthened the position
of Rome, as the champion of Orthodoxy, and she frequently
intervened in the disputes with decisive effect. On the other
hand in Eastern eyes, and in actual fact, the whole of the
West apart from the papacy and the Franks and Celts, was
Arian.

Then came Justinian's superb but futile attempt to turn
back the course of history. He recovered Africa from the
Vandals and by an immense effort restored Italy to the Empire
and marked the event by the Pragmatic Sanction in 554.
But Rome was in ruins and almost depopulated, as were many
other cities in Italy. Byzantium had not the strength to hold
what Justinian had reconquered. The Goths under Theodoric
had been able to protect the country and ensure an ordered
Roman life to the people. When Justinian's armies wiped them
out, Italy was left a prey to newcomers. No sooner was the
great Emperor dead than the Lombards fell upon it with a
savagery more intense than Italy had yet experienced.

Justinian's reconquest did nothing to draw East and West
together. Rather the reverse. Theoretically the Italians were
delivered from their Barbarian tyrants and taken once more to
the bosom of the "Roman" Empire. But the armies which
liberated them were largely composed of Barbarians, and the
sufferings of the people during the nineteen years' war were
immense. The men sent out to administer the country, the
functionaries and merchants who followed in the train of the

armies, were strangers from as far east as Syria, alien in every respect from the Romans of the West.

The Popes were treated in highly cavalier fashion once the need to use them in relation to the Goths had come to an end. The Emperor might receive Pope John II at Constantinople in 524 with the most profound gestures of veneration, and Pope Agapetus might even be allowed to depose on his own authority a Patriarch of Constantinople, during his stay in the Eastern capital ten years later. But when the imperial generals were masters of Old Rome, the Popes Silverus and Vigilius were treated in very different fashion (see page 40) and in the persons of its Pontiffs the Western Church was grossly humiliated.

It is not surprising that the Pope, beside being the chief bishop of Christendom, was often driven by mere force of circumstances to take the lead in secular affairs as well, and in that capacity to inherit something of the bygone glory of the Caesars. Nor is it surprising that his policy should develop into one which aimed at converting the Barbarians from their Arianism and making common cause with them against the Greek East. In point of fact, burdened with heavy commitments in the East, Byzantium could do little for the West, which was largely left to fend for itself, though the Empire in the West continued to exist in theory long after it had ceased to operate in fact. The Empire was immortal in men's thoughts, whatever vicissitudes it might suffer in historical fact. Heraclius after his Persian victory might have emulated Justinian and driven back the Lombards, but any such hope was shattered by the thunderbolt of Islam. The Lombards descended upon Italy in 568, and in a few years' time were masters of the north of the peninsula. They were for the most part Arians (though some were pagan) and as such added a special hostility to the Church to their normal ferocity.

With the Lombards nearing the very gates of Rome, Pope Pelagius II appealed to the Emperor for help. But this appeal from West to East for help in dire peril was as vain as the appeals which the East was to make to the new nations of the West centuries later in parallel circumstances. But Pelagius's successor was Gregory the Great. The administrative

D

experience and forceful character of this deeply religious and commanding personality were not long in making themselves felt in the Western Church as a whole. He took the Patrimonium in hand. The Patrimonium was composed of the lands belonging to the Roman Church. They were scattered in various places, notably in Sicily, and were of great extent. They made the Pope the largest landowner in Italy.

Gregory reorganized and consolidated the Patrimonium and that gave him a solid basis from which to take his part as need might be in secular affairs. And that was to no small extent. In 593 we find him conducting the defence of Rome when the Lombards were besieging it, as his counterpart the Patriarch Sergius was to be the soul of the defence of Constantinople in 626. Gregory was loyal to the Emperor, though he was not on good terms with him. The Emperor Maurice was, as usual, preoccupied with the East and was prepared to let Italy go. He suspected and disapproved of the Pope's policy, which was to secure some sort of pacification by coming to terms with the Barbarians, to make the most of the fact that the Lombard Queen was a Catholic and aim at converting the Lombards from their Arianism.

The mission of St. Augustine to England which Pope Gregory in his missionary zeal for souls had despatched in 596 may be regarded as a symbol, perhaps a premonition, of that which the inexorable movement of events was to usher in. For gradually the Pope's eyes came to turn towards the north, to the Catholic Franks, whose ruler was the greatest, in fact the only, effective power in the West. Under the impact of Islam, the stresses within the Empire were to give it two axes instead of one. And both axes ran northwards, the one from Rome through the Frankish territories to Britain, the other from the Balkans into Russia. But by that time there were two Emperors, for the Pope crowned Charlemagne on Christmas Day in the year 800. The details of this process lie outside the scope of this book, but the process itself must be noted as a dominant aspect of the drift apart of East and West and the coronation of Charlemagne as marking the climax of its political consummation.

We must return, however, to a brief consideration of another potent factor which operated in the same process. This was the Iconoclast Controversy, which in the eighth century shook the Eastern world and widened the breach between it and the West.

With the definite loss of Syria and Egypt the political reasons for the continual attempt to placate the heretics by doctrinal compromise disappeared, and in Baynes's words "the Empire could afford to be orthodox". The dogmatic decisions of the six Ecumenical Councils were accepted everywhere within the Empire. The new dispute was concerned with the traditions and customs of worship, with the use of "images", that is to say icons, pictures of sacred persons and scenes.

In the earliest days the use of painting and sculpture in connection with worship was but scanty. Its association with heathen rites caused it to be looked at askance by the Church, which inherited from Judaism a vivid consciousness of the perils of idolatry. But there are early frescoes in the catacombs, and from the fourth century onwards the feeling that the pictorial representation of sacred persons was to be feared and repudiated, subsided, and the tendency was to call upon the arts more and more for the embellishment of worship. The Peace of the Church brought increased opportunity for the building of new churches, and new wealth to provide for their adornment. The earliest icons which have survived, date from the end of the fifth or the beginning of the sixth century. The use of them spread rapidly and the attitude of the Church towards them at first seems fairly clear in the East and West alike. Gregory of Nyssa speaks of the silent painting speaking from the wall. And Pope Gregory the Great says that the use of them is to teach those who are unable to read. The Quinisext Council which met in 692 decreed in its 82nd Canon "that the figure in human form of the Lamb who taketh away the sin of the world, Christ our God, be henceforth exhibited in images, instead of the ancient lamb, so that all may understand by means of it the depths of the humiliation of the Word of God, and that we may recall to our memory His conversation in the flesh, His passion and salutary death, and His redemption which was wrought for the whole world."

Thus the function of the icons was twofold: they were to instruct, and they were to stimulate devotion. This latter function came to assume enormous proportions—and as the seventh century passed into the eighth the number of icons produced increased greatly. The subjects included not only pictures of Christ, Our Lady and the Saints, representations of incidents in the Old and New Testaments, but also scenes from the Apocryphal Gospels, pictures of martyrdoms and the like. The religious estimation in which the icons were held, particularly those of them to which a miraculous origin was attributed, those "not made by (human) hands", developed to an astounding and sometimes a fantastic extent. It passed, at times, into sheer superstition of a gross and material kind, and many people were much disquieted by it. Voices were heard declaring that the icons should be abolished altogether. The destruction of the "images" was to the iconoclasts an urgently needed reform to purge away idolatry and superstition, while to their defenders, the iconodules, it was a crude and wanton desecration of sacred things, sheer sacrilege and even a sign of heretical belief.

But one must beware of over simplifying the issue and of regarding iconoclasm as a mere expression of Puritanism. Historians have yet to reach agreement upon a balanced estimate of the motives which gave rise to the attack upon the icons. Some have thought it was due to the influence of the Jews or the Moslems, and this in spite of the fact that the Emperor Leo III, in whose reign iconoclasm as State policy began, was no friend of the Jews and had recently achieved a signal success against the Moslems. Others have seen it as part of the general programme of reform attributed to that Emperor, and especially as an attack upon the monasteries, which it certainly became later on.

Monasticism had, indeed, spread to vast proportions, and a statesman might well be disturbed by the loss to the exchequer from the immunity from taxation which the monasteries enjoyed, as well as by the loss of man-power to the army, the public services and the land which the increasing number of men who took the vows of religion involved. The monks, who made the icons and were their great defenders, exercised an enormous influence upon the populace. Thus, the controversy might be interpreted as due to a revolt of the laity against the spread of spiritual and especially monastic influence in directions held to be harmful to the interests of the community as a whole; or, from the opposite point of view, as an effort on the part of the Church to defend its freedom in the spiritual sphere.

The impulse to iconoclasm came from Asia Minor when two bishops took the initiative and endeavoured to persuade the Patriarch of Constantinople, Germanos, to accept their views. In the Eastern (now the most important) provinces of the Empire there was a strong feeling against the images, under the influence of the Jews, Moslems and possibly the Paulicians.[1] There had been a violent outbreak of iconoclasm at Antioch even in the sixth century, and half a dozen years before the Byzantine Emperor took any action, the Khalif Yezid had ordered the removal of all icons in the churches and houses of his Christian subjects. The army was largely recruited in Asia Minor, and was solidly behind the Emperor, himself a native of Isauria, and the Court party in their attack upon image worship. In defence of the images were ranged the bulk of the Western provinces, the majority of the clergy, the monks, and devout women (it is worth noting that the two sovereigns who restored the images, Irene and Theodora, were both women). The quarrel was between the Asiatic party in Constantinople, and the defenders of the Hellenistic traditions of the Empire.

There were two phases in the struggle, which it is not proposed to follow in detail here. The Emperor Leo III, the Isaurian, after some attempt at peaceful persuasion, launched his attack by ordering the destruction of the great icon of Christ over one of the gates of the imperial palace, a gesture which provoked an immediate riot and that in turn led to reprisals. His successor, Constantine V, besides being an iconoclast and hater of monks, was frankly heretical in other respects. He continued and intensified the attack his father

[1] On the Paulicians see Steven Runciman : *The Mediæval Manichee*, Camb., 1947, and Dmitri Obolensky : *The Bogomils*, Camb., 1948. The Paulicians were a Christian sect in Armenia and Asia Minor who had affinities with Gnostic Dualism and Manichaeism.

had begun and focused it especially upon the monastic order. A real persecution of the iconodules took place, and there were many cases of martyrdom. Constantine secured the support of a Council held at Hieria in 754, though neither Pope nor Patriarch (the See of Constantinople was vacant at the time) was represented at it. The Council condemned the cult of the images, but refused to be persuaded to condemn also the veneration of the saints and the belief that they intercede for men. Constantine's son, Leo IV, died in 780 after reigning only five years and his widow, Irene, who was a Greek of Athens, during the minority of his infant son, succeeded in restoring the cult of the images at the Second Council of Nicaea (the seventh Ecumenical Council) in 787.

This closed the first phase and a quarter of a century of uneasy peace followed. But the decisions of a council were not enough to calm the deep-seated passions which lay behind iconoclasm, and with the accession of Leo V, the Armenian, the quarrel broke out afresh. But this second phase of the struggle under Leo and his two successors Michael II and Theophilus shewed some marked differences from the former. For one thing the defenders of the images were not taken by surprise as they had been before. They were better organized with the centre of their dogmatic defence based upon the great monastery of Studium in Constantinople under its redoubtable Abbot Theodore who had already suffered exile as a prominent iconodule. Further there was not the same drive behind the iconoclastic movement in this second period, not the same enthusiastic support from the eastern provinces. There was a persecution and some martyrdoms under Leo V, but the two following emperors displayed much less zeal in the matter. Finally, and perhaps for these reasons, the second phase was shorter than the first by some twenty years, and another Empress, Theodora, restored the images again in 842, achieving in one year what had taken Irene seven. This time the victory was final and it has been celebrated ever since in the Orthodox Church by the annual observance of "Orthodox Sunday" on the first Sunday in Lent.

And, indeed, much was at stake. It was no mere matter of

the retention or otherwise of *objets de piété*, nor even of the value of the images as picture books in which the unlettered could read and learn their faith. Argument and counter-argument were exchanged on the terrain of the sin of idolatry. But the question was viewed at a deeper level still and notably by St. John Damascene who, from the safety of his position outside the Empire, wrote three treatises on the defence of the images in the time of Leo III. To him nothing less than belief in the truth of the Incarnation was involved. Since God took human flesh it is right and reasonable to depict that flesh. To the thorough-going iconoclast to use the material to represent the divine was blasphemous. It may well be that here we can trace the influence of Manichaeism, which taught that matter was essentially evil and that God did not truly assume human flesh at all: or, at least, of the Monophysites who held that the divine in Christ completely absorbed the human.

Vast numbers of works of art perished in the fury of the iconoclastic onslaught. On the other hand the artistic life of Southern Italy was enriched by the flood of immigrants escaping from the iconoclastic East, and in the East itself an incentive was provided for the ornamentation of churches with purely decorative forms of animals, of flowers and secular scenes, to which the iconoclasts had no objection.

To return to the special subject of this chapter. The iconoclastic controversy had an important bearing upon the loss of the West. At the outbreak of the struggle when Leo III failed to persuade either the Patriarch Germanos or the Pope to approve of his policy, he deposed the one and sent a naval expedition against the other. His fleet was destroyed by a storm. But the Emperor confiscated the revenues of the Papal lands in Calabria and Sicily to the imperial treasury, thus completing the political rupture between Byzantium and Italy. At the same time he transferred the ecclesiastical allegiance of the dioceses in the same regions as well as in Illyricum and Crete from the Pope to the Patriarch of Constantinople.

After the deposition of Germanos and Leo's appointment of an iconoclast Patriarch in his place, Rome was out of communion with Constantinople almost continuously for nearly fifty years.

And Charlemagne who was so shortly to become Emperor in the West had his say in the matter. A version (said to be made by someone who apparently knew neither Greek nor Latin) of the decrees of Nicaea II was sent to him. His reaction was prompt and definite. His case against the Council, perhaps drawn up by Alcuin in England, was sent to Pope Hadrian in the form known as the Caroline Books. It attacks the presumption of the Council in pretending to dictate to the Christian world, it attacks both the Council's doctrine of the Images and the iconoclast position, and how in any case, asks the Catholic Frank, can one trust people who say that the Holy Ghost proceeds from the Father alone?

CHAPTER IV

CONVERSION OF THE SLAVS

THE final breach between Rome and Constantinople still lay in the future. But to all intents and purposes Orthodoxy now stands alone, the religion of the Empire, and conceiving itself as the heir and guardian of the traditional Hellenistic culture. In the West the Papacy, still recognized as the primary see of Christendom, was virtually a secular power also, between the Empire and the Franks, with whom it was in close alliance and upon whose kings it had poured the anointing oil, and in the end bestowed an imperial diadem.

In the East the Melkite Patriarchates were isolated outposts within the fierce world of Islam which was battering at the defences of the Empire.

It was some compensation for those losses that Orthodoxy was able, in the ninth and tenth centuries, to initiate a great missionary achievement and to strengthen its position by securing the allegiance of the bulk of the Slavs. The inclusion of the Slavs within the orbit of Byzantium was not undisputed by Rome, and the rivalry was intertwined with other quarrels concerned both with jurisdiction and with doctrine which broke out between the two Churches in the ninth century.

The Balkans had been swept by successive waves of invaders, by the Visigoths, the Ostrogoths, and finally, as we have seen, by the Slavs and Bulgars, who established themselves there permanently, settling first in the open country, and later in the cities. The old civilization with its civil and ecclesiastical administration disappeared. But the Empire refused to regard the territory as permanently lost, it was still in theory a recoverable part of the Empire, and involved in the process of recovering it was the task of converting it to

Christianity. In districts where the primitive Slavs came into close touch with the Greek and Roman world and accepted its higher civilization and culture, they were far more easily induced to accept the Christian religion also, than was the case among the more remote masses of the invaders. These latter soon became aware of the fact that to embrace the new religion was a danger to their own tribal coherence and even to invite foreign domination in the political sphere.

There were other obstacles, too, which slowed down the process of converting the Slavs and Bulgars, and prominent among them the fact that ecclesiastical jurisdiction in the Balkans was a bone of contention between Rome and Constantinople. Politically the whole peninsula was part of the Eastern Empire, whether in fact or in theory. Ecclesiastically it had for centuries been divided between East and West. The geographical line of division had varied, but had tended to shift westward, and, as was recorded in the previous chapter, Leo III during the iconoclastic controversy had expelled Roman jurisdiction from Illyricum altogether. But this did not mean that the Papal claims in that respect were abandoned, and missionary enterprise for the conversion of the Slavs (including the Bulgars) came from the West as well as from the East. The invaders had by this time crystallized into various recognizable national units. There were the Moravians to the north, roughly in what is now Czechoslovakia; Slovenes in the south of Austria and the north-west of Yugoslavia; the Croats along the Dalmatian coast; the Serbs in the centre of the peninsula, and the Bulgars along the lower Danube.

The Slovenes having occasion to enlist the help of the Bavarians against their Avar enemies, came under the lordship of Bavaria, and later, with the Bavarians were engulfed in the Empire of Charlemagne. He drove out the Avars and incorporated both the Slovenes and the Croats of this region into the diocese of Salzburg. Thus they were converted from the Catholic West and later came under the direct control of the Pope. They have remained Roman Catholic to this day. The same is true of the Croats further south and along the Dalmatian Coast, though they showed some wavering between East and West in early days. For here, after the action of

Leo III above referred to, great efforts were made to induce the people to accept the Byzantine rite. But by the end of the ninth century the country had finally settled down to the Papal allegiance. Yet Mestrović's colossal figure of Gregory of Nin at Spalato stands as a witness to the long struggle of the Croats for the use of their Slavonic language in worship.

The Moravians also were destined in the end to come under the Roman obedience, although they owed their conversion largely to the Byzantines. And here we have the romantic story of Cyril and Methodius, two brothers who came to be known as the Apostles of the Slavs. They were Greeks of Thessalonika, men of great ability, the younger in particular (known in his lifetime as Constantine) having an established reputation as a teacher and philosopher in Constantinople. He had already been employed by Photius, before the latter became Patriarch, upon a political and religious mission to the Khazars, who lived on the plains through which the Dnieper and the Don flow into the Black Sea, and have the unique distinction of having adopted Judaism as their religion. While there Constantine acquired the relics of St. Clement of Rome, and apparently carried them with him on his later travels.

About the year 862, the Moravian Prince Rastislav sent emissaries to Constantinople, where they found Photius, now Patriarch, the most conspicuous figure. To counteract the danger of the recently formed alliance between Louis the German and the Bulgarians, Rastislav offered, and succeeded in establishing, his own pact with the Empire. The military side of this alliance bore fruit two years later when a Bulgarian army on its way to help Louis the German was defeated by the Byzantines.

There was an ecclesiastical aspect of the agreement also. Rastislav was restive under the vigorous nationalistic tendencies displayed by the German missionaries in his country: and to Photius the situation may well have seemed a valuable opportunity to strengthen his position against the Pope. Constantine and Methodius were despatched into Moravia where their efforts soon shewed signs of success, for they brought the Christian religion to the people in their own language. The brothers seem to have formed a happy combination, the elder with his gifts as administrator and the younger as scholar and linguist. And doubtless one of their main qualifications was that coming from Thessalonika, they had lived in close contact with a Slav population and were perfectly familiar with a Slav language.

It was presumably this Macedonian Slav dialect which the brothers reduced to writing and into which they translated a number of books, liturgical and other, for the use of their converts. They adapted the Greek minuscule letters into an alphabet to convey the Slavonic sounds, and this is the Glagolitic in which some old Church Slavonic was written and which, in a modified form, has survived for liturgical use still in certain dioceses on the Dalmatian coast. All the Orthodox Slavs today, however, use another alphabet, called Cyrillic, which is based upon the Greek uncials. Whether the Apostles of the Slavs had anything to do with the invention of the Cyrillic letters is uncertain—but they bear the name of the younger, for at the end of his life Constantine became a monk and took the name of Cyril. His death occurred in Rome in 869. Methodius went back as an Archbishop, to continue his labours in Moravia till his own death in 885.

The two brothers, with their devoted band of helpers, did an immense service for Slav religion and culture. But the attempt to set up a Slav Church in Moravia failed, and after the death of Methodius the Germanizing party secured the upper hand. Methodius's disciples and helpers were treated with some indignity and harshness and expelled. We shall meet them again later in Bulgaria.

The Serbian clans, lying inland, were less exposed than the Croats and Slovenes to outside influences, and although there was some infiltration of Christianity among them, no general conversion took place until the latter part of the ninth century. The Serbian Prince Mutimir, who died in 891, sent a request for missionaries from Constantinople and was himself baptized with large numbers of his people. But the political and utilitarian aspect of the event was rather unusually prominent. The Emperor had recently made a signal display of the might of Byzantine arms in his suppression of certain Serbian pirates in the Adriatic. It was not until the returning

disciples of Methodius made their influence felt that Christianity as religion made real progress among the Serbs, and
even so, many pagan customs were retained and, more or less,
blended with the new Faith. But the official conversion of
the Serbs is dated from the baptism of Mutimir. During his
reign the Serbian Church was under the direct influence of
Byzantium and the services were in Greek. But as Bulgarian
ascendency became predominant in the Balkans, Byzantine
suzerainty gradually gave place to Bulgarian, and the Greek
liturgy to the Slavonic.

The first Bulgarian king to receive baptism was Boris,
who reigned from 852 to 889 and was one of the ablest
monarchs in Bulgarian history. Christianity had penetrated
into Bulgaria before that time, and there had even been some
persecution of it, due largely to fear of it as an agent which
prepared the way for foreign and, in particular, for Byzantine
domination. Boris was a statesman and although his own
personal religious convictions played their part in his acceptance of Christianity, there were other considerations also
that he had in mind. To make his realm a Christian State was
some defence against the political and religious missionary
zeal of his Christian neighbours. Further, it would tend to
consolidate his own position. The great bulk of his subjects
were Slavs, and many of them already Christian; the Bulgars
were a ruling minority among whom Boris was the chief of
many rulers. To favour the Slav element in his realm, therefore,
and to Christianize it would be to break the power of the
Bulgarian nobility and establish himself as sole ruler with all
the force of the current Christian conception of royalty and the
divine authority delegated to kings, to support him. The revolt
of the Bulgarian nobles which subsequently broke out showed
that they realized all this clearly enough, but they were too
late.

In furtherance of his plans Boris looked first towards Rome
for the same reason that Rastislav of Moravia had looked to
Constantinople, i.e., each looked to the opponents of those
from whom their own danger was greatest. But the Byzantine
Emperor and Photius, then at the height of his quarrel with
the Pope, were just as much alive to the facts and struck first.

Boris found his country invaded and himself compelled to receive baptism at Greek hands. Accepting the situation, Boris now set himself to achieve the independence of the Bulgarian Church and with much astuteness availed himself of the bargaining power which the quarrel between Rome and Constantinople placed in his hands. He would have preferred to align himself with the West, and he made urgent and persistent efforts to induce the Pope to give him a Patriarch of his own. Pope Nicholas, who saw a chance of recovering for the Papacy the jurisdiction of which Leo III had deprived it, gladly sent Boris a couple of bishops, Latin service books and much good instruction (in answer to Boris's questions), but not a Patriarch. So Greek priests and books were turned out and Latin took their place and Boris continued patiently but urgently to press his request. But the Pope's star was in the ascendant, in 867 the Byzantine Emperor was assassinated, and the Patriarch Photius deposed. Feeling the ball at his feet the Pope ignored Boris's requests and adopted a high-handed policy towards him.

Boris lost patience and turned to Constantinople, which was ready enough to receive his overtures. But in view of the fact that a Council had been called to try to settle the differences between the two great sees, the question of the Bulgarian Church was submitted to it. The Council was packed with Eastern bishops, and in spite of the protests of the Papal legates who were present, naturally it was decided that the Bulgarian Church should be under the jurisdiction of Constantinople. An archbishop, with considerable independent powers, was appointed for Bulgaria. He was himself a Bulgar and with a train of bishops and priests he left for his archbishopric where once more everything Latin was replaced by Greek. Thus the victory in this affair remained with Constantinople. Not that the Papacy acquiesced in it. Much expostulation, many exhortations, and the sternest threats issued from the Pope, but no one paid any attention. But the time came when the sagacious Photius, now again Patriarch, thought it prudent to try to secure the Pope's recognition of his status. The Pope agreed provided that Bulgaria was restored to him.

The matter was once more submitted to a Council (in 879) which, surprisingly, decided that Bulgaria should be returned to Rome. But Boris refused to be returned to Rome. It is possible that this was a contingency which had been foreseen by Photius, but in any case he loyally abode by the agreement reached, sent no more clergy to Bulgaria, and remained on good terms with Nicholas's successor, John VIII. The final decision had, however, been reached and the Bulgarian Church was to remain within the orbit of Orthodoxy. One other aspect of Boris's policy remained to be realized. To make his Church a really national institution, worship must be in the language of the people, to whom the bewildering changes from Greek to Latin had meant but the substitution of one foreign language for another.

The disciples of Methodius, who had just been expelled from Moravia provided Boris with precisely what he needed. The less important of these unfortunate men had been dubbed heretics and sold as such into slavery, the more prominent leaders, Gorazd, Clement and others more politely conducted to the Danube and bidden to cross it, never to return.

Boris gave them a cordial welcome, and under his patronage they did a great work, far-reaching and permanent, for Slav Christianity and culture. A centre for the training of a Slav clergy was established, a Slav Bulgarian Church was organized, and many translations into the Slav language were made. Boris was wise and skilful enough to effect these changes without offending Byzantium and his own Greek hierarchy, and the latter were in due course replaced by Slav bishops. Thus through Clement of Okhrida and his companions the work of the Apostles of the Slavs bore a rich harvest among the Slavs of the Balkans. For the political ascendency of Bulgaria continued to grow until for a while it wrested the hegemony from Constantinople itself. Boris's successor, Simon, was an outstanding personality, who not only decisively defeated the Byzantines in war, and had himself crowned with an imperial title, but himself a scholar and erstwhile monk, carried on his father's ecclesiastical and cultural policy and declared the Bulgarian Church autocephalous. Thus was welded into shape in Bulgaria a cultural and religious instrument which was ready to hand when needed for the evangelization of Russia.

The Vikings, who were the terror of north-west Europe, made their way south-eastwards also, along the waterways which connect the Baltic with the Black Sea. Here they found a Slav population which about the middle of the ninth century was organizing itself in political centres such as Novgorod in the north and Kiev in the south. The Scandinavian warrior merchants passing from the Volkhov to the Dnieper, established themselves whether as protectors or conquerors as masters of these communities, and if *Russ* is indeed a Scandinavian word the process which took place in Bulgaria was repeated, and the ruling minority gave its name to the Slav people which absorbed them. These "Russians" soon found their way across the Black Sea to the Great City, Byzantium, known to them as Tsargrad. In 860 their fleet appeared beneath its walls but was dispersed by a tempest. The part of Sergius in 626 was on this occasion played by the Patriarch Photius, who inspired the defenders with courage and energy.

The early contacts of the Russians with Constantinople are shrouded in a good deal of obscurity, but certain events connected with their conversion stand out as historical. The Patriarch Ignatius sent an archbishop into the country and he made a number of conversions. Igor, Prince of Kiev, made an unsuccessful attack upon Constantinople in 941, and a treaty which he made with the Byzantine Emperor a few years later reveals the fact that there were then Christians at Kiev and that they had a cathedral dedicated to St. Elias. Whether this community was the direct descendant of the converts made by Ignatius, or derived its Christianity from elsewhere is unknown. Igor's widow, Olga, who was later canonized, was definitely a Christian. She visited Constantinople and may have been baptized either there or at Kiev, and at one time seems to have adopted the policy of Boris of Bulgaria and to have played East and West against each other in her ecclesiastical relations. In response to her request, a mission was actually sent from Germany by the Emperor Otto, but it was half-hearted, and returned without accomplishing anything. Neither Olga's son Svyatoslav nor her grandson were Christians but they at least tolerated Christianity, and Olga who lived until 969 was able to foster the growing Christian community.

It was Vladimir, an illegitimate son of Svyatoslav, who less than twenty years after Olga's death took the decisive step and accepted the new religion for himself and his people. He was lord of Novgorod and made himself master of Kiev. Much discussion has taken place about the circumstances of Vladimir's baptism and the relation in which that event stood to his marriage and his capture of Kherson.

Some scholars see no reason to look for any one external event as the occasion which brought about his baptism. He must have been familiar with the Christian religion and with the work of his paternal grandmother Olga, and it would not escape the attention of an intelligent man that while culture, civilization and political power were associated in his world with Christianity, paganism belonged to the half-barbarous hordes against whom he warred on the steppes. They therefore suppose that Vladimir was baptized in his own city of Kiev, before, or possibly during, the visit of an Embassy from Constantinople.

The more usual view is that the baptism took place at Kherson after Vladimir had captured that place, in the following circumstances. In Byzantium the imperial throne was being shaken by rebellion, and its occupants hard put to it to deal with the rebel. The Embassy was sent to solicit the military assistance of the Russian chieftain. It was successful, Vladimir's terms being good payment for his men and the hand in marriage of the Emperor's sister for himself. The terms were accepted, Vladimir carried out his part of the bargain, and with his help the rebellion was crushed. When the danger was over, however, the Emperors showed marked reluctance to let their sister go back with the victorious Russian, and Vladimir had to resort to force to secure possession of his bride. The walls of Constantinople were too strong even for his wild warriors, so on his way home he besieged and captured the Greek town of Kherson in the Crimea. This display of force proved sufficient to bring the Byzantines to reason, and the bride was forthwith despatched to her distant future home. She, with her ecclesiastical retinue from Constantinople, joined Vladimir

E

at Kherson. And thither also at the same time arrived an Embassy from Pope John XV.[1]

Vladimir set to work with energy to make his people Christian. The idols of the great god Perun and others, erected in not too distant a past (for Vladimir before he embraced Christianity had toyed with the idea of revitalizing the pagan religion) were overthrown and churches built in their place. The more or less instructed people were baptized in droves in the Dnieper. Other influences were at work beside that of Byzantine Orthodoxy. The institution of tithes is found in the early Russian Church, and it would seem that that must have come from the West, and the same is true of the veneration of certain distinctively Latin saints.

Even before the time of Vladimir, books and perhaps missionaries also had arrived from Bulgaria. The work which the disciples of the Apostles of the Slavs had carried on in that country spread into Russia, with the result that the Russian Church had a Slavonic liturgy from the beginning. After Vladimir's death there was a continued period of quarrelling among his sons, in the course of which the celebrated Boris and Gleb, unresisting, met their deaths. But one of the sons, Yaroslav, finally succeeded in establishing his position and reigning for thirty-five years. He it was who finally settled the dependence of the Russian Church upon the Ecumenical Patriarchate.

In 1037 Alexis the Studite consecrated Theopemptos as Metropolitan of Kiev and thereafter, with two notable exceptions, the Russian Metropolitans were Greeks appointed from Constantinople until the fall of that city. Yaroslav was a great lawgiver and he raised Kiev to a status in which he treated with European nations on equal terms and married his daughters into royal houses of the West. He built the superb cathedral of St. Sophia in Kiev and in his time the Petchersk Monastery was founded there. He died in 1054, the year in which the schism between Rome and Constantinople was finally consummated.

[1] On the puzzling question of the contact between the West and the Russian Church of this early period, see Dvornik, *The Making of Central and Eastern Europe*. London, 1949, p. 173 ff. and 255 f.

CHAPTER V

PHOTIUS AND CERULARIUS

THE story of the conversion of the Slavs in the ninth century was much entangled with the personal fortunes of Photius as Patriarch of Constantinople. That remarkable man was a scholar of immense erudition in many diverse fields of knowledge, and he occupied a conspicuous position in cultural circles in Constantinople, where as a layman he had held high office in the service of both the Emperor and the Patriarch Ignatius.

Few men have had such diverse judgments passed upon them as has Photius. The traditional view of the West has been one which regards him (in spite of his repeated assertions that he longed for a life of secluded study and accepted the Patriarchate against his inclination) as a man dominated by a passion for power, who stooped to lying, bribery and forgery to hold it, and as the real author of that schism between East and West which, although healed for a time, became final in the eleventh century.

Nevertheless, it is a Roman Catholic scholar who in recent years has undertaken his defence. Dvornik maintains that Photius has been grossly misrepresented in the West and that fuller knowledge of the facts of the case gives a portrait of the man more in accordance with the opinion of him held in the East, where he was long ago canonized and revered as a saint. 'If I am right in my conclusions," he writes, "we shall be free once more to recognize in Photius, a great Churchman, a learned humanist and a genuine Christian, generous enough to forgive his enemies, and to take the first step towards reconciliation."[1]

[1] Dvornik: *The Photian Schism*, Cambridge, 1948, p. 432.

In any case Photius's position is secure as an embodiment of classical learning and culture and as one of the greatest of the men who cherished and handed on to the future the tradition of Hellenistic life and thought which they had received from the past. In any case, too, the name of Photius became in the stress of later controversy a symbol; he and his writings became the expression of Orthodoxy, and the classical statement of the Eastern case against Rome.

His career must be viewed against the stormy background provided by the recurring dispute of parties in Byzantium. Party strife is a permanent feature which runs all through Byzantine history, dividing not merely the intellectuals but the whole populace into antagonistic sections, for the people of the city were passionately interested in theological questions. Dispute after dispute arose and was more or less settled, but the life of the parties continued and revealed itself again as new matters of controversy came to the fore. But as time went on such quarrels tend to become less and less purely theological, and more and more political. Controversies waged in the rarefied air of trinitarian and christological theology are replaced by the quarrel over the icons, which had but recently been settled when Photius comes upon the stage.

The old antagonism disclosed itself in a new feud concerned with the application of the moral law and the exercise of ecclesiastical discipline. The party which had been the champion of Orthodoxy against heresy and upheld image worship in the teeth of iconoclasm finds itself at odds with the hierarchy and the court on the question of the attitude of the Church to moral delinquency, real or alleged, in the imperial family. On the one hand, then, stands the extreme party, led by the monks of the Studium Monastery who held that a principle is best served by pressing it to its extreme logical conclusion, and insisted upon the rigorous enforcement of the moral law in every case alike. They found their supporters among the traditionally minded, the conservatives, people whose worldly position was reasonably secure and comfortable, who held to the old paths, devout people who feared that any concession would open up the way to laxity and undermine the established order in Church and State. They sympathized with those who thought it right to proceed to extremes against the iconoclasts, and their profound mistrust and even hatred of the study of the Hellenistic past and of profane learning in general was still another aspect of their general position.

There was a deep rift between them and the party of more moderate men, in closer touch on the one hand with secular intellectuals who viewed things from a more liberal standpoint and on the other with ordinary everyday life outside the cloister, where in the rough and tumble of living strict theory has sometimes perforce to give ground before the exigencies of practical experience. It was the opinion of these men that the best interests of the Church and of the moral law of which it is the appointed guardian, warranted, and on occasion demanded, some concession to human frailty, and that the stringency of the rigorists did not always in the long run serve the true interests of the ideal it sought to promote. Such a position was not without sympathisers among the parochial clergy, while it is easily understood that many of the bishops, part of whose responsibility was to translate theory into practical action, tended to view it with at least respect.

The situation was, therefore, highly complex, and any man who occupied the Patriarchal Throne had to take into account the many forms assumed by this permanent cleavage in Byzantine society. Indeed his accession to the see was usually the expression of the temporary ascendency of one party or the other, though many of the best of the Patriarchs were alive to their responsibility to try to reconcile contending factions and bring peace to the Church. Photius himself expressed a hope that his occupancy of the Patriarchal Throne would achieve such a result, though in fact it was far from doing so. His predecessor, Ignatius, a zealous and devout ascetic, but no scholar and of an unaccommodating mind belonged to, or at least allowed himself to be used by, the extremists. He fell foul of the imperial court by accepting, apparently on hearsay, the truth of current rumours of sexual immorality on the part of the Caesar Bardas, and by refusing him Communion. He was banished, and under pressure he resigned. Photius, still a layman, was elected in his place by the local synod and appointed by the Emperor, according to the usage of

Constantinople, and hurried through ordination to the various degrees of the sacred ministry within a week. He was enthroned on Christmas Day, 858. But the friends of Ignatius had no intention of accepting the position, and the Pope became involved in the dispute.

When any new occupant acceded to one of the five great Patriarchates it was the custom that he should notify the other four of his election and send them his profession of faith. This procedure was followed as usual by Photius, the most important notification being, of course, the intimation sent to the Pope. The Emperor also wrote to the Pope at the same time telling him what had happened at Constantinople, and inviting him to send legates to a Council which the Emperor was calling to secure a further pronouncement on the doctrine of the Images. Pope Nicholas, however, was suspicious. He was not sure that Ignatius had been justly treated; nor did he look favourably upon the rapidity with which Photius had passed from the status of layman to that of Patriarch. In spite of such cases as that of St. Ambrose, action such as this was regarded more seriously in the West than in the East. He sent legates, therefore, with strict orders to investigate, but no more, and they carried with them a letter to the Emperor which pointed out that the removal of Ignatius could not be recognized since it was done without the authorization of the Papal See; and the letter contained significant complaints about the Illyrian Sees which had been detached from the papal jurisdiction. The legates, however, were unable to resist the persuasiveness (whatever forms that may have assumed) of Photius and his friends.

More important than this was the fact that they, being in Constantinople, were in a position to see that the state of affairs there was in important respects not quite as it appeared in Rome where the persistent propaganda of the monk Theognostus on behalf of Ignatius was having its effect. They could have claimed a precedent for exceeding or even altering their instructions.[1] At any rate they consented to take part in a synod which condemned Ignatius and confirmed Photius in his position.

But the Pope still refused to make a definite pronouncement

[1] Dvornik: *The Photian Schism*, p. 90.

n favour of Photius, and the correspondence continued. Not until it became clear to the Pope that Byzantium would not yield in the matter of the Illyrian provinces did he decide. Then he came out vigorously on the side of Ignatius. A council was called at Rome, the legates, who on their first return from Constantinople had received no rebuke, were now punished for exceeding their instructions, and sentence of deposition was pronounced against Photius with the penalty of excommunication should he fail to yield up the See of Constantinople to its lawful occupant Ignatius. To these fulminations Photius made no reply, indeed no reply was called for from him, for since in the eyes of the Pope he did not exist as Patriarch, the letter was not addressed to him, but to the Emperor; the latter did reply in terms which the Pope said were blasphemous.

Yet a couple of years later the Pope set ajar once more the door that he had slammed so violently, and invited both parties to submit their case at Rome. But whatever hope of reconciliation lay in this gesture on the part of Nicholas, was wrecked on the Bulgarian question. The Pope was making desperate efforts to secure the young Bulgarian Church for the West. The Greek missionaries whom Boris had expelled (see p. 62) were streaming back to Constantinople when Photius startled the world by his famous letter of 867 addressed to the East at large. It complained in no measured terms of the Papal conduct in Bulgaria. He writes that the Bulgarians are being taught by the Papal mission to fast on Saturdays, and allowed to use milk, butter and cheese in the early days of Lent. Other strictures concerned matters of greater moment, such as the desire to enforce celibacy upon all the clergy and the alleged refusal to recognize confirmation administered after the Eastern fashion by the priest immediately after baptism, with oil consecrated by the Bishop.

The letter summoned the Eastern prelates to a Council which should proclaim their condemnation of all these deviations from Orthodoxy. The Council did indeed assemble at Constantinople that same year. It provided an overwhelming majority in support of Photius, and even went to the length of pronouncing the deposition and excommunication of the Pope. Photius claimed that he had the support of certain bishops in the West and there was even an attempt to turn the Franks against the Pontiff, and an offer of the title *Basileus* to Louis II, which may suggest that the Council looked to him in return to give effect to its decisions and eject the Pope. It was a moment of Byzantine triumph. The Emperor had recently won a great victory over Islam to match the Patriarch's triumph over the Pope, the missions among the Slavs were prospering. The Eastern Patriarchs were solidly behind Photius, and precisely at this juncture the great Pope Nicholas died. But precisely at this juncture also, Photius fell, swept away in the wake of a palace revolution which overthrew the Emperor Michael III.

Ignatius was recalled to the Patriarchal Throne and peace was made with Rome under Nicholas's successor, Hadrian II. Another Council was convened in 869. Photius was condemned, but not even now would Constantinople yield on the Bulgarian question, which was indeed vital to Byzantium from the political point of view, all ecclesiastical questions apart, for Bulgaria was a next-door neighbour. Nor could the extremist party continue to hold the ground it had won. The new Emperor Basil began to modify his policy towards Rome and the West, there was a reconciliation between him and Photius, and it would seem that the latter was personally on good terms with Ignatius also. The latter died in 877 and Photius reascended the Throne of Constantinople. Still another Council was assembled which, in 879, reversed the decision of ten years earlier. Photius remained Patriarch until another change of sovereign ejected him again, and this time finally. His attitude was conciliatory to Pope John VIII, who recognized him as Patriarch. He was even ready to compromise on the matter of Bulgaria, and it was not his fault if the Bulgarians themselves insisted on remaining Orthodox. But the Eastern grievances against "innovations" introduced by the West both in matters of discipline and in doctrine remained, and prominent among them was the question of the *filioque*. Photius himself wrote much on this subject. No less than thirty-one arguments against the use of the *filioque* may be collected from his writings.[1]

[1] A summary statement of them is in Gavin : *Eastern Orthodox Thought*, p. 129 ff. London, 1923.

In the West when the Creed which is commonly called Nicene is recited, the belief is expressed that the Holy Ghost proceeds from the Father *and the Son*. The last three words, in Latin *filioque*, do not occur in the Creed as used in the Orthodox East. They form no part of the original Creed as it first appears in Acts of the Council of Chalcedon 451, where it is attributed to the Second Ecumenical Council. The *filioque* arose and spread rapidly in the west of Europe and particularly in Spain, where it made a very effective weapon in combating the Arianism of the Barbarians. It appeared in the Creed as recited at the Council of Toledo in 589 and this fact contributed to its widespread use in Spain and Gaul. It was the Franks who were the great champions of the *filioque*, and it was long before the Pope was persuaded to adopt it at Rome. He had not done so at the time of the Photian controversy. It was not introduced into the Creed at Rome indeed until 1014. It is clear, therefore, that the East had, and has, legitimate grounds of complaint that the phrase was introduced into the Church's Creed irregularly and without the authority and consent of the whole Church. It is important to observe that the Eastern rejection of the *filioque* rests primarily upon the fact that it is an unauthorized innovation.

But Photius maintained and the Orthodox have always believed not only that the words are irregularly inserted into the Creed, but that they are in themselves untrue. It must be clearly noted that as used in the Creed the *filioque* does not refer to the temporal mediating of the Holy Spirit to this world. If that were so the Orthodox would agree that although invalid in the Creed the words are true in fact. But the reference is to the timeless being of the Trinity, to the very nature of the Godhead, and it is to the disproof of the truth of the *filioque* in that respect that the thirty-one arguments of Photius are directed. Remote as so subtle and transcendent a mystery might seem to be from human concerns, the *filioque* has figured prominently in the relations between East and West, and has furnished material for learned and often acrimonious debate from the days of Photius to the Bonn Conference in 1874. The Orthodox allow that the phrase "through the Son" might be permissible as an opinion, but they will not tolerate a form of

words which seems to them to suggest the possibility that two
Sources, Causes or Originating Principles exist within the
Godhead.

It was an uneasy peace between Constantinople and Rome
which followed the Photian affair. The Byzantines felt all the
while that they were faced by a two-headed foe. Over against
their Patriarch, the Bishop of the Imperial City, the New
Rome, inheritor and guardian of the treasures of the past in
civilization and religious faith, stood the Pope with his claim
to universal jurisdiction in the Church. Over against their
Emperor stood the ruler of the Franks who had assumed the
title Emperor of the Romans, and for the Byzantines there
could in the nature of things be but one Emperor, and he the
occupant of the throne of Constantine.

It was a shock to read such words as Louis II had written
to the Emperor Basil urging that it was no matter for surprise
if the writer calls himself Emperor of the Romans, rather than
of the Franks. It was the Church of the old Rome which had
conferred the imperial title upon his family, and it was his
mission to defend and exalt the Mother of all the Churches.
The Greeks had ceased to be Emperors of the Romans because
of their heresies and moreover they had forsaken the city and
seat of Empire for another city, another people and another
language.[1]

At much the same time a Pope had written "stop calling
yourself Emperor of the Romans, since these Romans are from
your point of view merely Barbarians." As for the bishops
of Constantinople and Jerusalem, although the title of Patriarch
has been conceded to them they have not the same authority—
"No apostle founded the Church of Constantinople: the
Council of Nicaea makes no mention of it. It is only because
Constantinople is called New Rome, and more due to the
favour of princes than of right, that its bishop has assumed the
title of Patriarch."[2] Here indeed was a radical difference in
outlook which would call for much charity to adjust, charity
which was not always in evidence. Moreover, in the tenth
century the Papacy fell upon evil days and presented a series

[1] Lavisse et Rambaud : *Histoire Générale*, Vol. I, p. 656. Paris.
[2] Ibid., p. 657.

of Popes who from the moral point of view may be simply described as bad. Although by the middle of the next century the turning point had been reached and the great Popes Hildebrand and Leo IX were inaugurating the reforming movement which was to change the face of the West, by the time Michael Cerularius ascended the Patriarchal Throne of Constantinople in 1043 the Byzantines had grown accustomed to looking upon the Papacy with justifiable apprehension.

Opening the campaign indirectly through Leo, Bishop of Okhrida, Cerularius in 1053 launched a general attack upon the West. Some of the slogans inscribed upon the banners carried into the fray seem today to be almost incredibly trivial. The *filioque* was scarcely mentioned, the Western enforcement of clerical celibacy was dwelt upon, and the East attributed this to the intrusion of Manichaean ideas; but it provides some food for thought that a disaster of such dimensions as the Schism could be made to rest even ostensibly upon a list of charges in which such matters as fasting on Saturdays and the use of unleavened bread in the Eucharist figure with some prominence. The conflict was short and violent.

The Pope, Leo IX, answered with much indignation in a letter which, while replying to the Patriarch's accusation and making counter accusations of his own, strongly asserted the claim that the Roman see "must hold the primacy over the four sees of Alexandria, Antioch, Jerusalem and Constantinople as well as over the Churches of God throughout the whole world."

Soon afterwards the Pope died, just as his predecessor Nicholas I had died at the climax of his dispute with Photius. But meanwhile he had despatched legates to Constantinople, one of whom was Cardinal Humbert, a learned man who was in the forefront of the controversy on the Papal side. He knew Greek but whatever the language he was not accustomed to choose his words with any great regard for the feelings of his opponents, nor was he given to compromise.

The Emperor, Constantine X, had no desire to break with the Pope, whose military alliance he needed against the Normans in Sicily, and he welcomed the legates graciously. His power was enough to guarantee the personal safety of the legates, but could do no more to counter the will of the formidable Patriarch who would have nothing to do with them. On July 16, 1054, the Papal legates deposited on the altar of St. Sophia a bull of excommunication against (not the whole Eastern Church, but) the Patriarch and his adherents.

In vain had the Patriarch of Antioch counselled Cerularius to be patient "with the Barbarians". Whatever virtues Cerularius had, patience was not conspicuous among them; and the fact that the sincere and general opinion in the East was that the Latins were Barbarians, and in the West that the Easterns were schismatics, was one of the deep-rooted causes of the trouble.

In the event, Peter of Antioch and the other Eastern Orthodox hierarchs stood by Constantinople, and the West remained unshaken in its loyalty to the Pope. Historians have remarked that at the time the breach seemed to attract little attention. The two great sees had so often been out of communion before that no doubt it was supposed that the schism would in due course be healed again. But this time it was to last, and to bring vast evils in its train.

The worst effects of the schism were the intensification of the fundamental causes which had brought it about. Each side held the more tenaciously to its own position, the isolation one from the other was deepened, their paths became the more divergent, each went upon its own way. Animosity grew more marked, and if the mere lapse of time tended to soften this into indifference and suspicion, yet it was ready to flare up again at any moment.

Attempts were made from time to time to repair the breach. But they all came to nothing. It is easier to tear one's coat than to mend it. The Pope desired reunion, but only on his own terms. The enhancement of the power of the Papacy and its increasing centralization, after the Cluniac reform of the monasteries and the Pope's decisive victory over the Emperor, gave him confidence to insist upon his conditions. In the East there was no desire for reunion for its own sake, but only a vivid sense of how useful it would be; and this, though it might carry the day at a Conference, proved an inadequate incentive for the Orthodox as a whole to accept the Western terms.

Political events moved in directions which emphasized for intelligent men the urgent need for unity, but at the same time in the actual course they took hindered rather than promoted it. The Orthodox world was through centuries the great bulwark of Europe against Asia, and in fulfilling this function it needed the military as well as the moral support of the West. It was in the teeth of the secular authority that Cerularius had precipitated the quarrel, and the Emperor Constantine remained on friendly terms with the Pope. This aspect of the Crusades must be borne in mind. That romantic episode in Christian history, a great ideal which became a great disillusionment, was on the one hand a war for the recovery of the Holy Places and to render them safe for Christian pilgrims to visit. On the other hand it arose from a letter which the Byzantine Emperor, Michael VII, wrote in 1073 to Pope Hildebrand appealing for help against the Turks and promising ecclesiastical reunion of East and West in return. The Pope responded favourably and himself issued an appeal to the faithful of the West to go to the assistance of "the Christian Empire, against the pagans who have now carried their devastation almost to the walls of Constantinople." The project of rescuing the Holy Places was an afterthought.

Further cries for help from the hard-pressed East led to renewal of the appeal by another Pope, Urban II, twenty years later, and the response to this became the First Crusade. But the Crusades achieved nothing good in the relations of East and West. To the turbulent hordes of enthusiastic Crusaders the Greeks were primarily "schismatics" whatever might be their shock of surprise to discover the wealth and civilization of Constantinople. The Greeks complained vigorously of the disorderly conduct of the Crusaders and the insolent ignoring of the Emperor's rights in their setting up of Latin kingdoms in the East. The Crusaders on the other hand were loud and bitter in their resentment of the lying and treachery with which they said they were treated.

All this bad feeling culminated in the unspeakable infamy of the Fourth Crusade. In 1204 a crusading army sacked the Christian city of Constantinople with every circumstance of horror, barbarity and sacrilege. The memory of this burnt deep into the Eastern mind and it was the behaviour of the Crusaders more than any other single circumstance which made the breach between East and West permanent. A puppet Latin Empire was set up in Constantinople, while the authentic line of the Eastern Emperors continued to function across the straits at Nicaea, until in 1261 Michael VIII returned to Constantinople where the restored Eastern Empire, although grievously wounded, maintained its life for another two centuries.

Against such a background of secular experience it is hardly surprising that well-meant and even eager attempts to reunite the Churches, came to nothing. A synod was held at Bari in 1098. The acts have been lost and our knowledge of the proceedings is derived from Eadmer's life of St. Anselm of Canterbury, who played a prominent part in them, undertaking the defence of the *filioque*. It is assumed that the Eastern point of view was represented solely by Greek bishops from Southern Italy. Under strong political pressure the Council accepted the Western position upon all the points at issue, including Papal jurisdiction; but there the matter ended. The Council of Bari, it will be noted, was held long before the Crusaders' sack of Constantinople, and if that Council failed to have any permanent effect, it was not probable that the Council of Lyons (1274), only seventy years after the sack, would be any more successful. But at first it looked more hopeful. Constantinople was officially represented by three distinguished envoys sent by the Emperor, but the Patriarch of Constantinople refused to have part or lot in the matter. There was no great discussion; within a few weeks the Eastern representatives agreed to everything. Reunion was proclaimed. The Eastern Emperor replaced his recalcitrant Patriarch by one who favoured reunion, and set to work to try to enforce the bargain of Lyons. He did his best, although the Pope excommunicated him for not doing better. But he died without being able to induce his Church and people to accept the agreement reached at Lyons, and his successor openly repudiated it.

It was nearly two centuries later that the greatest and most famous of the "Reunion Councils" was held at Florence in 1439. Meanwhile, the Turkish menace was becoming ever more insistent. The Empire had weakened, it lost its supremacy at sea, and it had also to face the rise of the Bulgarian and Serbian powers in Europe. It had lost much of its trade to Venice and Genoa. By the time of Florence the Turkish tide was half-way across Asia Minor, by 1353 they had reached its western coasts and crossed into Europe. Adrianople was captured and the Turks made it their capital and from it proceeded to their attack upon the Serbs and Hungarians. The southern Slavs were completely crushed at the disastrous battle of Kossovo in 1389 when the Serbs and their allies under Lazar were wiped out. Constantinople was becoming an island fortress, proud and Christian in the ever-encroaching sea of Islam.

Negotiations were continuously taking place with the object of securing aid from the West. It was always the same story. The West was prepared at times to use force and at times to be accommodating. For using his influence to bring succour to Constantinople, the Pope's price was always the same. And whatever was in their hearts about reunion, the Eastern Emperors were prepared to pay the price. Time and again they agreed to yield in the matter of Papal jurisdiction, the *filioque*, unleavened bread and the rest. But the Church and the bulk of the people would not support them. With the memory of 1204 still vivid their feeling was—better the Turk if needs must than the Pope.

The Council of Florence was, however, distinguished from the Council of Lyons by the fact that at the former the Easterns were officially represented by envoys duly accredited from the Patriarchates of the East and not merely sent by the Emperor. Indeed the Patriarch of Constantinople was present in person (he died while the Council was meeting) and in addition to representatives from Alexandria, Antioch and Jerusalem and a score of other bishops, the Metropolitan of Kiev came from Russia. There were long and stormy debates, but the end was as before. The Easterns, all except Mark of Ephesus, who refused to sign, once more accepted the *filioque*, unleavened bread and the rest, including the Papal Primacy; though the Pope, himself anxious to bring matters to a close, accepted an acknowledgment of the claims which contained the phrase "without prejudice to the privileges and rights of the Patriarchs of the East."

So the union was proclaimed with due thanksgiving. Even in England the bells of all the parish churches were rung to celebrate the event. But it brought no military aid to the dying Empire, save a few hundred men sent by the Pope himself. The Pope could no longer bring effective influence to bear upon the mutually jealous Western powers to unite them in defence of Constantinople. The Eastern delegates on their return were execrated by Church and people and their action was repudiated. Mark of Ephesus was acclaimed as the hero of Orthodoxy. Yet in theory the union survived the fall of Constantinople, and the last Emperor who exclaimed "I will die with my city", died in communion with Rome. The victorious Turk found it to his interest that his new Christian subjects should not be on friendly terms with the military powers of the West. The union was formally denounced at a synod in Constantinople in 1472.

With the notable exception of Russia, and of Crete, which was held by the Venetians till 1669, the Orthodox world had now to live its life under the rule of the Turks until the nineteenth century.

CHAPTER VI

ORTHODOXY IN BONDAGE

THE Sword of Damocles fell at last, and the menace which had hung over Eastern Christendom for centuries became the realized fate of the Orthodox peoples for centuries more. The armies of Islam swept over the Balkan peninsula and sub-merged it, though the city of Constantinople itself still stood inviolate.

In the year 1389 the battle of Kossovo was fought which decided the fate of Serbia, and brought its mediaeval glory to an end. A page of history was turned over. It was a page upon which the name of Sava had been inscribed, the national Saint of Serbia, prince, monk, educationalist and organizer of the Serbian Church, and the names of the saints and leaders of the Serbian Church who succeeded him. Upon it was recorded the achievements of the Serbian Empire in the first half of the fourteenth century, when the warrior Dushan struck terror into the hearts of his neighbours and at their expense brought wide territories under his sway. He was a lawgiver and administrator too, a stern dispenser of justice. On that same page is described the precocious civilization and enlight-ened culture of Dubrovnik, known otherwise as Ragusa, which in the fourteenth century, Miss Waring tells us,[1] had "a city police and sanitary board", as well as men of letters and exponents of the arts. And Dubrovnik if pre-eminent was not alone, as the mediaeval churches of Serbia and their furnishings testify.

The battle of Kossovo brought the Serbian Empire to an end. But in the minds of the Serbs themselves it also revealed

[1] L. F. Waring : *Serbia*. London, 1917 (Home University Library), p. 154.

F

the idealism of the Serbian spirit at its highest point. For the night before the battle the Serbian Tsar had a vision in which he was offered the choice between an earthly and a heavenly crown. He chose the heavenly and rode out to the conflict and his own death on the morrow, knowing that from the earthly point of view all was already lost. There is something truly Orthodox here and especially perhaps Slav Orthodox, for Russian religion, too, is permeated by reverence for suffering in body or mind and a sense of its regenerating power.[1] It is this dark day of Kossovo which has become the National Day of the Serbian people. Day of utter defeat and obliteration of earthly hope as it was Kossovo Day has been observed ever since as a yearly memorial of the greatness of the past, and an occasion of self-dedication to the Serbia of the future.

But the new chapter of Balkan history which immediately follows bears the record of the Turk whose rule was marked by casual neglect, haphazard uncertainty and ingenious brutality.

The City of Constantine held fast for another sixty years. Then its walls were breached, and in the breach the last Byzantine Emperor died. Mahomet, the conqueror, rode to Justinian's Church of the Holy Wisdom where he dismounted and entered. He stopped the pillage that had already begun, and caused a passage from the Koran to be read from the pulpit.

For good and evil, Christian Byzantium had played out its part at the meeting place of East and West. Alexander's *Drang nach Osten* had come back like a flowing tide.

The story of the Orthodox Church under the Turkish régime is one to excite both admiration and pity. The Turkish point of view must be grasped. They drew no distinction between nationality and religion, to them secular and religious politics were one and the same. This might be said of the Byzantine Empire too, but with a difference. Within the latter, there was a Church distinct from, and it might be, opposed to, the State. The Turkish armies sallied out with the con-

[1] Cf. Gorodetzky : *The Humiliated Christ in Modern Russian Thought,* London, 1938.

viction that the world was to be subdued to Islam. If the people they conquered were simple pagans they were offered the crisp alternative of accepting either Islam or death. But the Jews and the Christians were different. They were recognized as being, like the Mohammedans themselves, People of the Book. Each had a scripture, a written record of revelation. Their faith was regarded by the Turks as true but incomplete, since Mahomet had superseded both Moses and Christ.

The Orthodox were, therefore, permitted to survive and to practise their religion, but under severe restrictions. They had to pay tribute, to wear a distinctive dress and to conform to other irritating and humiliating regulations. In practising their religion they had to refrain from letting any outward sign of it be seen or heard, there were to be no crosses, for instance, on their churches, and no bells were to be rung. All this was the letter of the Law, nor was there any guarantee that it would be adhered to by the victorious Turkish governors; indeed, it was often violated by a harsh sultan or a blood-thirsty local administrator. There was much suffering and many instances of martyrdom. Doubtless there were many cases of apostasy also.[1] Social pressure was a more effective agent in winning converts to Islam than deliberate oppression and direct official action.[2] Its results are to be seen in the atrophy of the Christian Church in North Africa, and in the considerable number of adherents which Islam gained at the expense of Christianity in the Balkans.

But it is the glory of the Orthodox people as a whole that under centuries of Turkish oppression and misrule, with every inducement to abandon their religion, they remained faithful to it in spite of all.

For purposes of administration under the Turks the Orthodox Church became the *Rum Millet*—the Roman nation, with the Ecumenical Patriarch as its recognized head and representative. That is to say the Patriarch of Constantinople

[1] See Latourette : *A History of the Expansion of Christianity*, Vol. III, p. 71 and f. London, 1945.
[2] It has been discovered in modern Russia that religion is like a nail, the harder you hit it, the deeper it goes in, and that the subtler policy of leaving social pressure to do its work is the wisest course for those who hope to see the disappearance of religion.

was given civil jurisdiction over all the Orthodox within the Turkish Empire; he was responsible for their behaviour, they could approach the Government only through him. Thus, to his former claim to ecclesiastical precedence over the other Eastern Patriarchs, was now added a delegated civil jurisdiction as well.

The result was a signal example of the corrupting influence of power. The temptation to use secular authority as a means to ecclesiastical aggrandizement was strong, and it is one of the ironies of history that the Turkish régime led to the steady expansion of the spiritual jurisdiction of the Patriarchate of Constantinople. It reached its climax in the eighteenth century when the Churches of Rumania, Bulgaria and Serbia were brought under its sway and the Patriarchate extended right across Asia Minor. But the price paid was seen in the Patriarch's relation with his Turkish masters.

He was obliged to receive his "berat" from an infidel source, that is the confirmation of both his spiritual and secular authority. He was removed, and sometimes more than once reinstated, at the Sultan's will, and this combination of humiliating loss of prestige with the prize of rich emoluments led to a long and depressing story of simony and intrigue. There have been notable exceptions and some Patriarchs have suffered deprivation and even death for their principles. But over long periods of time the acquisition and tenure of the Patriarchate was a matter of intrigue and money, and the precarious nature of the dignity is reflected in the fact that "out of 159 Patriarchs who have held office between the fifteenth and twentieth centuries, the Turks have, on 105 occasions, driven Patriarchs from their throne; there have been 27 abdications, often involuntary; 6 Patriarchs have suffered violent deaths by hanging, poisoning or drowning; and only 21 have died natural deaths while in office."[1] During the seventy-five years from 1625 to 1700, there were 50 Patriarchs—an average of eighteen months each.[2]

Nor was the evil limited to the Patriarchate itself. The party which had bought the office for their nominee recovered

---

[1] Kidd : *The Churches of Eastern Christendom* (1927), p. 304.
[2] Fortescue : *The Orthodox Eastern Church* (1907), p. 242.

their expenses, through him, from the Greek bishops whom he appointed to the sees within his vast jurisdiction. They in their turn passed on the burden to their parochial clergy, who finally reimbursed themselves from their parishioners in the Balkans and Asia Minor.

It must be remembered that the level of education and culture really was higher among the Greek clergy of the Phanar[1] than among the Bulgars, Serbs and Rumanians, and to that extent there was good reason for appointing Greek bishops in those "daughter" Churches. But it is not surprising that the system, especially in its fiscal aspect, gave rise to much resentment, and that when in the nineteenth century the Balkan peoples began to recover their political independence from the Turks, they were equally eager to escape from their ecclesiastical dependence upon Constantinople. This movement met with its first success in 1833 when the Church of the Kingdom of Greece declared its independence, though it had to wait seventeen years for its recognition by Constantinople. The Serbian Church followed suit in 1879 and the Rumanian in 1885. These independent Churches were established not without struggle and a good deal of friction, but at least they have remained in full communion with Constantinople. In the case of Bulgaria, however, it led to schism. The Bulgars claimed more than ecclesiastical independence within a defined locality, i.e., the Kingdom of Bulgaria; they insisted that the head of the Bulgarian Church must have jurisdiction over all Bulgars wherever they may live. This the Phanar would not agree to, and branded it as the heresy of "Phyletism".[2] In 1872 the Ecumenical Patriarch, with the concurrence of the other Patriarchs, except Cyril of Jerusalem, excommunicated the Bulgars, and the Schism remained till 1945.

Nothing perhaps more clearly illustrates the isolation into which the East was driven by the Schism of 1054 and the Turkish conquest than the fact that it had no part in the making or opposing of the Reformation, that great cataclysm which shook and split, and yet revivified, the Western Church in the

[1] The seat of the Patriarchate in Constantinople from 1586 onwards.
[2] Exaggerated emphasis upon the spirit of nationality in the ecclesiastical sphere.

sixteenth century. That is not to say that the Reformation had
no effect at all upon the East. Its repercussions were felt there
in the following century, and about this something must now
be said. It is connected with the person of Cyril Lucar, a
remarkable and tragic figure, whose personality and writings
dominated Orthodoxy in the seventeenth century. He was
born in Crete, which was then still under Venetian rule, in
1572. It was to Venice, and also Padua, that he went as a
student, after which he settled in Alexandria, where he was
ordained, became an Archimandrite and took his place in the
immediate entourage of the Patriarch. In due course the latter
sent him on a mission to Poland, the purpose of which seems
to have been to try to persuade the Protestants in that country
to become Orthodox. It was a fateful journey for Lucar, for
while there he became attracted to Lutheran and Calvinist
doctrines and followed the trail of them to Wittenberg and
Geneva.

On his return he succeeded his late patron who died in
1603, and became Patriarch of Alexandria. Seventeen years
later he was made Patriarch of Constantinople and continued
so intermittently till his death in 1638. His tenure of that high
office is a conspicuous example of the insecurity that attached
to it under the Turkish régime, for he was six times deposed
and as often reinstated during those years. Both at Alexandria
and at Constantinople Lucar made vigorous and persistent
efforts to popularize the ideas which had aroused his enthusiasm
in the West, and to establish a reforming movement within the
Orthodox Church on the same lines as had been adopted by
the Western Reformers. With the co-operation of the Chaplain
to the Dutch Embassy at Constantinople he started a Protestant school in that city, and put out a Greek version of the
Bible which he had printed at Geneva and which bore evident
doctrinal marks of its place of origin. He conceived and carried
out a plan for sending promising theological students to study
in Switzerland, Holland and England, the best known of them
being Metrophanes Kritopoulos (himself later Patriarch of
Alexandria) who was sent to Balliol College, Oxford. Lucar's
relations with this country are of great interest. He corresponded with Abbot, Archbishop of Canterbury; and the

fifth century manuscript of the Bible, known as Codex Alexandrinus which is one of the most precious treasures of the British Museum, was presented by Lucar to Charles I from the Library of Alexandria.

This strange figure of a Protestant Patriarch encountered violent opposition. Not only had he to face the solid uncompromising body of traditional Orthodoxy, he was met also by the bitter hostility of the Jesuits and of a Latinizing party within his own Church which had been formed by the proselytizing efforts of Roman Catholic missions. These were very active at the time, and enjoyed the support of France and Venice.

In 1629, Lucar published his celebrated *Confession*, a document which contained much Calvinist doctrine and inaugurated a controversy which was not settled until the Synod of Jerusalem in 1672. Lucar himself was strangled by order of the Sultan on a trumped-up charge which his enemies brought against him. Just how far Cyril Lucar himself was a "heretic" has been disputed. It has been maintained that he did not hold the doctrines attributed to him, and the assertion of the Synod of Jerusalem that he did not write the *Confession* has been repeated by modern writers.[1] A synod held at Constantinople the year after his death condemned both Lucar and the *Confession*; the following Synods of Jassy and Jerusalem the *Confession* only. What is certain is that the Orthodox Church rose in a body to repudiate Lutheran, Calvinist or any other sort of "Protestant innovations"—whether Lucar held them or not.

The Synod of Jerusalem (sometimes called the Synod of Bethlehem, because it was convoked from that place) is of very great importance. It was convened with the express purpose of condemning the *Confession* attributed to Lucar but in doing so it promulgated a positive affirmation of the faith of the Orthodox Church.[2] Its acts include a Confession of Faith which "is a closely knit, carefully worked out summary of theological doctrine, in its phraseology very strongly

[1] E.g., Mesolora, and others. See Gavin : *Greek Orthodox Thought*, footnote on pp. 214 ff.
[2] The Acts of the Synod of Justin, and Cyril's *Confession* may be found in English in J. N. W. B. Robertson : *The Synod of Jerusalem*, 1899.

impregnated with scholastic terminology and in the exactness of its language and dialectical distinction refreshingly clear and lucid."[1] It is known as the *Confession of Dositheus* and is one of the "Symbolic Books" of Orthodoxy.

There are important doctrines of the Church, such as the theology of Grace, the Church, the Sacraments, and Justification, which were not dealt with in the seven Ecumenical Councils and upon which Orthodoxy made its pronouncements after the Schism, and mainly in the synods of the seventeenth century when the need arose for the Orthodox Church to define its position in relation to the teaching of the West, both Roman Catholic and Protestant.

The Symbolic Books of Orthodoxy are expositions of the belief of the Orthodox Church written by various authors on various occasions which called for them, and subsequently recognized by ecclesiastical authority.

The teaching of these books, though not on the level of the decrees of the Ecumenical Councils, are received throughout Orthodoxy as of very great authority, particularly because they are held to express nothing which is not consonant with the Ecumenical Councils and the writings of the Fathers. There are five Symbolical Books, and with the exception of the first they all came into being as a result of the Reformation. They are:

1. *The Confession of Gennadius Scholarius*. This was written by the Gennadius who became Patriarch of Constantinople in 1454. He wrote it as an exposition of the Christian Faith for the use of Moslems.

2. *The Three Answers of the Patriarch Jeremiah II* (1576, 1579, 1581). These are the Orthodox side of a correspondence between Jeremiah, Patriarch of Constantinople, and certain Lutheran theologians of Tübingen who brought him a Greek translation of the *Confession of Augsburg* and suggested negotiations with a view to reunion.

3. *The Confession of Metrophanes Kritopoulos*. Before Kritopoulos became Patriarch of Alexandria in 1630, he travelled in Germany and England (see page 86). While in Helmstadt in 1625 he wrote this *Confession*, setting forth the

[1] Gavin, p. 216.

enets of the Orthodox Church as compared with both Roman
Catholicism and Protestantism, for the benefit of his Lutheran
friends who had asked him to do so.

4. *The Orthodox Confession of Mogila.* Peter Mogila was
Metropolitan of Kiev, 1632–46. His *Confession* is written in
catechetical form, and received the approval of more than one
synod. It was revised and in its final form has the signatures
of the Four Patriarchs and many other hierarchs.

5. *The Acts of the Synod of Jerusalem* (1672) and *the
Confession of Dositheus* which was promulgated with them.
Dositheus was the Patriarch of Jerusalem at the time and he
presided at the Council. This Synod of Jerusalem (or Bethlehem) was the most important of the group of synods which
were convened as a result of the alleged *Confession* of Cyril
Lucar (see page 87). There were three others beside Jerusalem,
i.e., Constantinople (1638) Jassy (1641) and Constantinople
(1672).

The Synod of Jerusalem is of great significance for the
modern exposition of the faith of the Orthodox Church, and
it will be of interest to look at its proceedings more closely.
The Synod was concerned in the first place to assert that Cyril
Lucar did not write the *Confession* attributed to him, and to
support this contention by citations of other utterances which
were undoubtedly his and were, in the view of the Synod,
inconsistent with passages in his alleged *Confession*.

Nevertheless, so eager was the Synod to repudiate the
teaching of this document and to deny that it expressed the
teaching of the Orthodox Church, that it incorporated in its
own Acts those of the Synod of Constantinople in 1638,
which had anathematized Cyril by name. This was done on
the ground that Cyril had survived the publication of the
Confession for six years, and yet had not written against it,
although he had often been begged to do so. His verbal
repudiation of certain passages in the *Confession* were held to be
insufficient, and the Synod of Jerusalem confirmed his condemnation "if he was, indeed, a heretic and did not repent."

The Synod refers all who wish to know what the Orthodox
Church teaches to the Answers of Jeremiah and the *Confession*
of Mogila, and then adds its own exposition of the faith. This

is the *Confession* of Dositheus, which takes the form of 1 decrees and 4 questions dealing one by one with the 1 chapters and 4 questions of Cyril's *Confession*, in conjunctio with which therefore they should be read to be fully under stood. The *Confession* of Dositheus bears seventy signature beside his own.

The first of the Decrees is a brief statement of the doctrin of the Holy Trinity. "Cyril" had said that the Holy Ghos proceeds from the Father through the Son.[1] The second deal with the Holy Scriptures, which ought to be believed "withou doubting yet not otherwise than the Catholic Church hat interpreted and delivered the same."[2] Then follow Decree which state the Orthodox doctrine as opposed to Lutheranism and Calvinism on such matters as Predestination, Origina Sin, and Free Will. "We believe the most good God to hav from eternity predestinated unto glory those whom He hat chosen, and to have consigned unto condemnation those whon He hath rejected; but not so that He would justify the one and consign and condemn the other without cause. For tha were contrary to the nature of God who is the common Fathe of all, and no respecter of persons, and would have all men to be saved, and to come to the knowledge of the truth; but sinc He foreknew the one would make a right use of their free-will and the other a wrong, He predestinated the one, or condemne the other." Decree 13 states very clearly the necessity of bot Faith and Works: "We believe a man to be not simply justifie through faith alone, but through faith which worketh throug love, that is to say, through faith and works. But (the notion that faith fulfilling the function of a hand layeth hold on th righteousness which is Christ, and applieth it unto us fo salvation, we know to be far from all Orthodoxy." The Churc is taught and illuminated by the Holy Spirit, not, however immediately "but through the Holy Fathers and Leaders o the Catholic Church." (Decree 12.) Indeed "the dignity o the Bishop is so necessary in the Church, that without him neither Church nor Christian could either be or be spoken of

[1] The Synod of Jassy which also dealt with "Cyril's" chapters seriatir apparently takes this as equivalent to the *filioque*. Unlike Jerusalen Jassy did not condemn Cyril personally, but only the alleged *Confession*.
[2] The quotations are from Robertson : *Synod of Jerusalem*, 1899.

For he, as a successor of the Apostles, having received in continued succession by the imposition of hands and the invocation of the All-holy Spirit the grace that is given him of the Lord of binding and loosing, is a living image of God upon the earth." (Decree 10.)

Decree 15 is concerned with the Sacraments and 16 and 17 with Baptism and the Eucharist in particular. The Sacraments, called "Mysteries" by the Orthodox, are seven in number, to accept any other number of sacraments is "heretical madness". They are: Baptism; Confirmation or Holy Chrism, which was instituted by the words "Tarry ye in the city of Jerusalem until ye be endowed with power from on high"; Holy Orders, which was instituted by the words "This do ye for my memorial" and the words "Whatsoever ye shall bind or loose upon the earth shall be bound or loosed in the heavens"; the Eucharist; Marriage; Penance; and Unction—"the Holy Oil or Prayer Oil is spoken of in Mark and is expressly witnessed to by the Lord's brother."[1] In general, the Sacraments have "something natural" and "something supernatural". They are not "bare signs of the promises of God", but "efficient means of grace to the receivers", and "we reject as something abominable and pernicious the notion that when faith is weak the integrity of the Mystery is impaired."

It is to be observed that the Decrees of the Synod of Jerusalem, and particularly the 17th and 18th, carry what Neale called "a clear taint of Latinism". They belong to a period when the influence of Rome was strong in the Orthodox Church, and of all the authoritative formulae of Orthodoxy they reveal that influence at the highest. For instance, the 17th Article on the subject of the Eucharist uses the word transubstantiation and employs the terminology of substance and accidents. "We believe," it says, "the Lord Jesus Christ to be present, not typically, nor figuratively . . . but truly and really, so that after the consecration of the bread and the wine the bread is transmuted, transubstantiated, converted and transformed into the True Body Itself of the Lord which was born in Bethlehem of the ever-Virgin." "Further, we believe that after the consecration of the bread and wine there no

---

[1] St. Mark vi, 13. St. James v, 14.

longer remaineth the substance of the bread and the wine
but the Body Itself and the Blood of the Lord under the
species and form of bread and wine; that is to say under the
accidents of the bread." "Further, that the Body Itself of the
Lord and the Blood That are in the Mystery of the Eucharist
ought to be honoured in the highest manner, and adored with
latria. For one is the adoration of the Holy Trinity, and of the
Body and Blood of the Lord. Further, that it is true and
propitiatory Sacrifice offered for all Orthodox, living and dead,
and for the benefit of all, as is set forth expressly in the prayers
of the Mystery delivered to the Church by the Apostles, in
accordance with the command they received of the Lord.
Further, that before Its use, immediately after the consecration,
and after Its use, What is reserved in the Sacred Pyxes for the
communion of those that are about to depart (i.e., the dying) is
the true Body of the Lord, and not in the least different there-
from; so that before Its use after the consecration, in Its use,
and after Its use, It is in all respects the true Body of the Lord."
"Further, that this Mystery of the Sacred Eucharist can be
performed by none other, except only by an Orthodox Priest
who hath received his priesthood from an Orthodox and
Canonical Bishop in accordance with the teaching of the
Eastern Church."

The sacramental doctrine of the Orthodox Church is,
therefore, the same as that of the Catholic West. But there is
this important fact to be noted. This same 17th Decree expressly
states that the word transubstantiation is used not to explain
the manner of the change but to express and emphasize the
reality of the fact of it. Gavin[1] quotes Chrysostom Papado-
poulos as saying "the influence of Latin theology was entirely
external and ought not to be over-emphasized. This superficial
similarity of expression in its teaching ought not to be regarded
as identity in thought." That is to say that the Orthodox use
of the word transubstantiation to express the fact of the change
need not be held to commit the Easterns to acceptance of the
scholastic philosophy to explain the manner of the change.

It is significant that when the Acts of the Synod of Jerusalem were translated into Russian and published in 1838,

[1] p. 217, footnote.

onsiderable alterations in phraseology were made: the more
obvious Latinisms and in particular the reference to substance
nd accidents were excised.[1]

The 18th Decree of the Synod of Jerusalem is concerned
vith the state of the departed and with prayers on their behalf.
After death, souls enter into joy or misery according to their
ctions in this life. But neither the joy nor the misery is complete until after the General Resurrection. The souls of those
vho have sinned mortally but have repented before death,
"though without bringing forth any fruits of repentance"
descend into Hades and there endure punishment. "But
hey are aware of their future release from thence and are
delivered by the Supreme Goodness through the prayers of
he Priests and the good works which the relatives of each
do for their Departed; especially the unbloody Sacrifice."
The word Purgatory is not mentioned. The wording of this
Decree is also slightly modified in the Russian version. And,
ndeed, the general conception which seems to control the
Orthodox mind on this matter, is of the Church as the body
of the faithful whose life is upheld by mutual prayer and
ntercession. The death of the body is irrelevant. All the
departed, from the Blessed Virgin Mary to one's own parents
may be prayed for, and prayed to. If a man can ask for the
prayers of someone he knows on earth, there is no reason why
he should cease to do so after that person has died, nor is his
physical death any reason why he should cease to be prayed
or.[2]

The Questions appended to the Decrees are the same as
hose attached to "Cyril's" *Confession*. 1. Ought the Divine
Scriptures to be read in the vulgar tongue by all Christians?
2. Are the Scriptures plain to all Christians that read them?
3. What books do you call Sacred Scripture? 4. How ought we
to think of the Holy Icons and of the Adoration of the Saints?

---

[1] See a translation of the Russian text with comparison with the Greek
of Decree 17 in Neale : *History of the Holy Eastern Church*, London, 1850,
Vol. II, p. 1173. And an interesting report of a conversation with Philaret
of Moscow on the Russian use of the word transubstantiation in Headlam :
History, Authority and Archeology, p. 199, note 2. London, 1909.

[2] See Khomyakov's well-known poem printed in Birkbeck : *Russia and
the English Church*, Vol. I, p. 2. London, 1895.

The Synod's Answer to the first three is that the Scripture "should not be read by all but only by those who with fitting research have inquired into the deep things of the Spirit," and who understand how they should be read. The New Testament itself is quoted to shew that the Scriptures "are very profound and their sense lofty; and that they need learned and divine men to search out their true meaning." It is asserted that the Books of the Apocrypha are genuine parts of Scripture.

In answer to Question 4, "Cyril" had said, ". . . We permit those that so desire to have icons of Christ and the Saints; but the worship and service of them . . . we reject." The Synod, however, gives an answer of some length and reasserts the doctrine of Icons affirmed by the Seventh Ecumenical Council (see p. 54) and refers to that Council by name. It draws a clear distinction between worship as *latria* which may be offered to God alone, and the *dulia* with which the Saints and their icons are adored, or rather honoured. There is further a higher degree of *dulia*, called *hyperdulia* which is paid to the Blessed Virgin Mary, "the Mother of God the Word. For though, indeed, the Theotokos be servant of the Only God, yet it is also His Mother as having borne in the flesh one of the Trinity; wherefore also she is hymned as being beyond compare, above as well all Angels as as Saints; wherefore also we pay her the adoration of *hyperdulia*."

Finally the *Confession of Dositheus* appeals by name to a number of writers who have written expositions of the Orthodox Faith, to the Fathers, to the Ecumenical Councils, as expressing the same teaching as the Confession. And even the heretics, it says, Nestorians, Armenians, Copts and the Ethiopians, apart "from their own particular heresies" believe the same thing

A few years before this Council of Jerusalem assembled Macarius, the 147th Patriarch of Antioch, had returned from a journey to Moscow. It was his second visit to that city. He had been there before in 1655, when his son Paul, Archdeacon of Aleppo, had accompanied him, and kept a diary which is full of interest and at times diverting.[2] He made his journeys

---

[1] The Russian version omits this : and tones down somewhat the refusal of permission to all to read the Scriptures.

[2] Ridding : *The Travels of Macarius*. London, 1936.

pparently in defiance of the Sultan's general order which
orbade such travel without his leave, and one account says
hat the Sultan hanged him on his return; but the matter is
bscure. The reasons for his visits to Russia, however, are
lear enough. In the first place he went to collect alms for his
lock, whom Turkish misrule had reduced to the last extremity
f misery and debt. Russia was at this time the only Orthodox
and under Christian rule, and it is rather pathetically referred
o as "the land of the Christians" by one Oddib who celebrated
n verse his master the Patriarch's return. Macarius's second
ourney was undertaken in company with Paisius, the Patriarch
f Alexandria, to take part in the Council which tried and
leposed Nikon of Moscow in 1666.

To the Orthodox in bondage under Moslem rule, Russia
ppeared as a far off land of promise, a place of rest and peace,
vhere Orthodoxy was free and honoured. And it is to Russia
hat we too must now turn.

CHAPTER VII

RUSSIA

THE important fact about Russian civilization is that it is Byzantine in its origin, and that in spite of what Toynbee refers to as Russia's "fits of Westernization", its convulsions due to the injection of ideas from the West, (e.g., under Peter the Great), and again in its adoption of Marxism, Byzantine it has remained.

If anyone cares to dispute this about Russian civilization as a whole, he can hardly do so about the Russian Church in particular. In the eleventh century the Russians, or rather their Scandinavian rulers, took over Orthodoxy as one whole thing from Constantinople. It was the reverse process of what happened in the Roman Empire when the State adopted Christianity after it had largely won the people. In Russia the princes accepted Christianity and then gradually imposed it upon their subjects. Christianity had a thousand years' experience behind it, and Orthodoxy had reached its final form when Russia embraced it. No disputes about fundamental Christian doctrines disturbed the Russian Church. The Trinitarian and Christological controversies were settled, the marriage of Christian revelation with Greek philosophy had been consummated, and the conflict to settle the relations between religion and art had been fought out. Together with the liturgical books and all the external apparatus of worship, Russia took over a fixed body of doctrine, a monastic system, a style of building and ornamenting churches, and a body of legal principles.

In all these matters Russia was to introduce modifications and to set a Russian stamp upon them, for in spite of its method of adoption Orthodoxy entered into the soul of the

Russian people and became its very life. But the Byzantine character of Russian religion was conserved. As we have already seen the Russian Church was for long dependent upon Constantinople. Its literature consisted of translations or imitations of Byzantine writings. Its Metropolitan was a Greek consecrated in Constantinople and sent to rule the Russian Church. The two exceptions provided by the appointment in Russia of Hilarion in 1051 and Clement in 1147 are regarded as isolated cases which did not impair the theory and change the practice, which held good till 1448.

Politically the Russians lived for a century and a half under Mongol domination. From the battle of Kalka in 1223 the onslaughts of these mysterious, hideous and inhuman hordes, suddenly appearing from whence no man knew, burning, killing, capturing, had struck terror into the hearts of the dwellers on the Russian plain. Kiev, the cradle of Russian Christianity, the ancient and beautiful stronghold on the Dnieper, was sacked in 1240, and one by one the rest of the Russian towns speedily succumbed. Novgorod alone escaped, protected by its remote situation behind its marshes and forests, and by the courage, self-sacrifice and political wisdom of its prince, St. Alexander Nevsky. The Tartar rule bore less heavily upon the Church than upon the State. When their victory was assured the Tartars were at first, in matters of religion, easy-going pagans, and so long as they received their tribute, did not interfere unduly with the religion of the people they conquered. And as was also to be the case later on with the Balkan peoples under the Turk, it was their religion and their Church which, in the days of social and political disaster, saved the Russians from complete despair and preserved among them some sense of fundamental unity in spite of all their factions and divisions.

The Russian Church was the nurse of the growing national spirit of Russia. In the person of one of its great national saints, Sergius of Radonezh, who founded the Monastery of the Holy Trinity near Moscow, for centuries the citadel of Russian religion and national aspiration, it inspired the movement which thrust back the Tartar domination. In 1380 Dmitry of the Don, whose building of stone walls round Moscow had been a challenging gesture to which the Tartars were not slow

G

to respond, came to seek the advice of St. Sergius and received the calm assurance: "Go forward and fear not, God will be with thee." Everything was at stake, including Russian religion, for the Tartars had by this time embraced Islam, and their easy-going tolerance of Christianity was a thing of the past. The hard-fought wavering battle of Kulikovo Pole followed and ended in a Russian victory, and the beginning of the end of the Tartar dominance.

Much missionary activity was displayed by the Russian Church during the period of Tartar domination. Even among the Tartars themselves this evangelistic work was carried on, while many a lonely outpost of monastic life in the forests and swamps of the north spread the faith of Christ in regions where it had been unknown before. Few names of individual pioneers have been handed down, but among them is that of the energetic missionary bishop, Stephen of Perm.

After the fall of Kiev, the centre of gravity in Russian life, both political and ecclesiastical, had moved northwards, first to Vladimir and finally to Moscow, around which Ivan the Great and his son Vasili IV built up the Tsardom of Muscovy at the close of the Tartar period.

It was at first but a small area in the centre of what is modern European Russia. Kiev and the south were not under its control, nor did it extend to the Baltic. It had no port until the commercial enterprise of the Englishman, Richard Chancellor and his fellow traders, provided one at Archangel in the sixteenth century. But to the east expansion was to prove surprisingly easy, the counterflow to the Tartar invasion swept into Siberia under Yermak towards the end of the sixteenth century, and the colonists that followed bringing the life and religion of Russia were soon to reach the shores of the Pacific.

But to return to the fifteenth century, the Tsardom of Moscow was for long to remain the only Orthodox Christian realm free from foreign and non-Christian suzerainty, and it became aware of itself as the heir of Constantinople. Nor were the Russians unwilling to see their Church play the leading rôle in Orthodox Christendom. From their point of view Constantinople had deserved its fate, for its act of apostasy in accepting the terms of Union at Florence. A Greek named

Isidore had been appointed by the Patriarch of Constantinople to be Metropolitan of Moscow. Isidore represented the Russian Church at Florence and in company with the other Easterns (except Mark of Ephesus) he signed the Act of Union, which two years later, on his leisurely return to Moscow, he caused to be solemnly read at the Liturgy in the Uspensky Cathedral. The response of his flock was to arrest him and imprison him in a monastery. He escaped and fled to Rome and the Russians elected their own Metropolitan in his place. The fact that Constantinople accepted, even for a time only, the Florentine terms of Union which the Russians themselves so energetically repudiated, convinced them that Constantinople had betrayed the Orthodox Faith, and the fall of that city so soon afterwards seemed to them to set the seal of divine approval upon their judgment.

It is a matter of some surprise that the Russian Church was content to remain for so long a period in its dependent position and did not claim its autocephalicity until 1448. Long before that date the number of its bishops far exceeded what was required for a Church to become autocephalous. Its adherents were ethnically different from those of its mother Church, and the difference of language between them must have been a source of difficulty. Politically the Russians owed allegiance to their Tsar, and were not subjects of Constantinople. Geographically they were far removed from the administrative centre of the mother Church and communication involved much expenditure of time, considerable inconvenience and some danger. There would seem then to be ample grounds for the independence of the Russian Church to be claimed and granted long before it was. On the other hand there were clear advantages accruing from the fact that the Metropolitan was a Greek who came from abroad and owed ecclesiastical allegiance outside Russian territory. It enabled him with impartiality and with better hope of success to mediate in the constant feuds which rent the early Russian State. It assisted the Church to play its part as peacemaker and a unifying power. The Russian princes themselves were often wise enough to recognize this.

A Russian writer[1] has recently claimed the reverence of

---

[1] S. Troitsky in the *Journal of the Moscow Patriarchate*, July, 1948.

the Russians for ecclesiastical law as a further reason for the delayed independence of the Russian Church. For the canons require the consent of the mother Church before the daughter can become autocephalous, and Constantinople was reluctant to give this consent. "The income which Constantinople received from the broad and rich Metropoly of Russia formed a huge item in the Patriarchal budget." It is, however, not fair to assume that Constantinople was actuated entirely by mercenary motives. However that may be, in the end the Russians took the matter into their own hands, regarding themselves as absolved from their canonical obedience by the fact that in their view Constantinople had lapsed into heresy by accepting the Union of Florence.[1]

Thus the fall of Constantinople in 1453 and the submergence of the Balkans beneath the flood of Turkish invasion, roughly coincided with the emergence of Russia from beneath the yoke of the Tartars. As Orthodoxy was eclipsed in the south, it arose with new strength and splendour in the north and Moscow picked up the torch which fell from the dying hand of Constantinople. The legend of "Moscow the Third Rome" came to birth as the inspiration and expression of this renewal of life and ambition among the Russians after their long experience of depression under the Mongols, and brought with it a sense of their responsibility for the future destiny of Orthodoxy in history and of a Russian mission to the world. The message of the monk Philotheus to the Tsar Vasili III (1505 to 1533) assuring him that although two Romes had fallen a third had risen in the north which should never pass away, and acclaiming him as the supreme and only Christian ruler in the world, long haunted the minds of the Russians, and was expressly endorsed by the Stoglav Council in 1551 (see below, p. 101). A surprising ancestry was discovered for the Russian ruler, whose line of descent was traced back to the imperial house of ancient Rome, if not beyond. Correspondingly he assumed the imperial title, he became Tsar (Caesar) and "autocrat".

[1] According to the writer just quoted the Russians did apply in due form for the consent of Constantinople to the consecration of their nominee Jonah as Metropolitan of Moscow in 1448, but there is no evidence that any reply was received.

Thus Church and State developed side by side and often worked harmoniously together. As time went on, however, the Metropolitan came to be more and more dependent upon the Tsar, who on more than one occasion dispensed with the form of election altogether and frankly appointed his chief bishop himself, a course of action for which Constantinople had supplied precedents. A case in point is that of the Metropolitan Daniel, and it is involved in the controversy between the Possessors and the Non-possessors which divided ecclesiastics in sixteenth-century Russia.

The Non-possessors desired a reform of the monasteries and in particular disapproved of the possession of landed property by monks whose vow of poverty, they held, should apply corporately as well as individually. They were led by scholars and mystics like Maxim the Greek and Nil Sorsky. The Possessors, under Joseph of Volokalamsk, while holding the opposite opinion on the subject of monastic property, were supporters of the steadily increasing autocracy of the Tsar, whereas their opponents took a more liberal and humane view both about the authority of the State and about the exercise of discipline upon heretics, whom Joseph and his friends felt little compunction in calling upon the secular arm to destroy. The Tsar Vasili III was childless and proposed to divorce his wife and marry another woman. The Metropolitan Barlaam whose sympathies inclined to the Non-possessors refused to sanction this or to perform the ceremony. He paid for his principles by life imprisonment in a monastery, and a pliant Possessor was found in the person of Daniel whom Vasili made Metropolitan in his place and by whom the new marriage was solemnized. Moralists have not failed to point out that the fruit of this marriage was Ivan the Terrible.

The dispute between the Possessors and Non-possessors went on. Some legal adjustments were introduced into the hitherto unrestricted right to bequeath lands to the religious houses. The celebrated Council of the Hundred Chapters or Stoglav[1] which met in 1551 enacted certain reforming measures,

[1] *Sto* means one hundred, and *glav* means chapter. The enactments of the Council were divided into a hundred chapters. Hence the name Stoglav, which is applied both to the document and to the Council which produced it.

some of which were concerned with the monastic life. But the core of the Council was conservative and it set the seal of its sanction upon the general pattern of Russian life. It authorized a revision of the Service books, though little came of the authorization. It pronounced in favour of the old Russian customs in making the sign of the Cross and the singing of Alleluia. All these were matters which were to give much trouble to the Patriarch Nikon later on (see below, p. 103).

The differences between the Possessors and Non-possessors on the ethical and humanitarian sides of their controversy remained unresolved, and in general Nil Sorsky failed to establish the ideals he desired in Russian monastic life, and to secure the acceptance of more humane principles in the treatment of heretics. In this respect perhaps he lived before his time. More than a century later two deacons whose wives had died of the plague had forsaken their ministry and married again. They were sent to prison to be kept without food until they perished, and only escaped this fate through the special intercession of the Patriarch of Antioch who was in Moscow at the time.

As the power and dignity of the Russian Tsar increased, it seemed but fitting that his chief bishop should have a corresponding status and receive the supreme ecclesiastical title. With little difficulty this was achieved in 1589 and the title of Patriarch of Moscow was conferred upon the Metropolitan Job and subsequently recognized by the other Eastern Patriarchs.

Thus Russia became the fifth Patriarchate of the Church and was held, in some sense, to have taken the place of Rome which had "fallen away". The assumption of this new dignity was accompanied by the creation of a number of new Russian dioceses, and the raising of others to Metropolitan rank.

A generation later Russia again lay under the heel of an invader. The period of disturbances and civil war known as the Troublous Times brought with it foreign invasion. The Poles overran Russia and were in possession of Moscow. For sixteen months they had been laying siege to the famous Monastery of the Holy Trinity a few miles away. Then a dramatic episode occurred. In response to letters sent out from

he Monastery a great patriotic host came to its rescue under
he leadership of a prince, a butcher, a monk and a Cossack,
lrove out the Poles, and established Michael as the first Tsar
)f the House of Romanov and his father Philaret as Patriarch.
The House of Romanov was to last until the collapse of imperial
Russia, and the advent of the Soviets. The Patriarchate was
1ot so long lived. But in addition to Philaret himself it produced
t least one outstanding figure in the vigorous personality of
Nikon.

Nikon, of peasant origin, was a rigorist, vigorous and
lominating, sincere and ascetic. As head of the Chudov
nonastery in Moscow he had been the close friend and adviser
)f the Tsar Alexis, the devout son and successor of Michael,
or some years, when in 1652 with a good deal of reluctance
nd some stipulations he yielded to the Tsar's entreaties and
ccepted the Patriarchal Throne. Perhaps he foresaw that his
)wn personality and conception of his duty as Patriarch were
)ound to clash with those of his friend and sovereign. Such in
act proved to be the case. Nikon felt himself bound in con-
scince to resist the encroachments of the secular power in the
ealm of spiritual affairs. But at the same time he had little
scruple about intruding his own will into secular matters,
vhere his harsh severity and arrogance made him many
:nemies among the boyars.

There was another aspect of the troubles which were to
gather around Nikon and in the end overwhelm him. It was
he question of the revision of the Service books of the Church
—a thorny matter on which many men both in Russia and
:lsewhere have pricked their fingers.

The Old Slavonic books used by the Russian Church had
)een translated from the Greek, and in the course of centuries
)f transcribing, minor errors had inadvertently crept into the
:ext. Beside these matters there were other questions in dispute,
such as whether the sign of the Cross should be made with
:wo fingers in the Russian manner or with three as the Greeks
were accustomed to make it. And how often should Alleluia
)e sung on certain occasions? One may be pardoned some
astonishment at the fury of the passions aroused by the mere
discussion of these subjects. But this is to misunderstand. Men

were not fighting about trivialities as such. In a sense nothing
in the sphere of religion was a triviality. It is to overlook
the fundamental fact that Orthodoxy was, and is, regarded
by the Orthodox as one whole thing. To a man like
Avvakum,[1] Orthodoxy, doctrine, rites, ceremonial, painting
and music was one integrated whole. The slightest change in
any detail was a breach in the fabric of Orthodoxy—and no
such breach was to be tolerated at any price.

The question was not new in Nikon's day. A century before
under Ivan the Terrible an attempt had been made to revise
the Service books, and earlier still a learned Greek monk
named Maxim had been brought to Moscow to undertake
the work. The extraordinary history of that unhappy man
reveals the intractable nature of the task in the atmosphere of
ignorance, prejudice and passion which enveloped it. He came
to Russia, as an invited guest, to carry out a work of scholarship.
He spent thirty-eight years in Russia, twenty-six of them in
captivity and sixteen in an actual dungeon, and for a long while
excommunicate.

It did not ease the difficulty that the only standard by
which the Russian books could be corrected was the corresponding Greek books. Russian ecclesiastics did not know
Greek, and few, if any, wanted to know it. The Greeks were
suspect, living now in the land of the infidel, and had they not
surrendered to Western heresy at Florence, for which the
judgment of God had swiftly overtaken them in 1453? Moscow
was now the torch-bearer and champion of Orthodoxy, the
third and final Rome, the guardian of the true faith.

No improvement in the Service books emerged from all
this high feeling, and the matter cropped up again when
Nikon became Patriarch. By nature an ardent reformer he
would reform not only men but books.

The presence of Macarius the Patriarch of Antioch and
his suite in Moscow presented an opportunity of which the
Russian Patriarch was not slow to take advantage. Both
informally and formally in a synod summoned for the purpose,
he compared the Russian practice with the Greek and always
accepted the latter as correcting the former, and the rulings

[1] See page 105.

of the Greek visitors were acquiesced in. This did not add to Nikon's already scanty popularity, especially when he proclaimed with more honesty than tact: "I am a Russian and the son of a Russian but my faith and religion are Greek."

Even Avvakum had been prepared to amend the Russian books from the older Slavonic editions and manuscripts. But that was before Nikon's day as Patriarch, and when the latter proposed to appeal to the Greeks as the criterion, Avvakum and his friends from being moderate reformers went into the most violent and unappeasable opposition.

Avvakum was a remarkable man and he could write. He was in fact the most outstanding figure in Russian literature before Peter the Great. His autobiography which has been translated into English, should certainly be read. He defied the authorities with implacable obstinacy, goaded them with virulent abuse, suffered untold hardships as a consequence and in the end won the martyr's crown which he so eagerly desired.

In due course, the conflict between the ecclesiastical authorities and Avvakum's party (for he had many friends and sympathizers) developed into an open schism which has persisted to this day. Thus Russian Dissent, unlike English, owes its origin to opposition to reform, not to the advocacy of it. The Old Believers, as the dissenting party was called, became highly fissiparous and sometimes most eccentric. They suffered much persecution over a long period of time. "But on the whole," to quote Prince Mirsky,[1] "they have been the truest —in many cases the only—preservers of pre-Petrine Russian civilization. Were it not for them our contemporaries would hardly have rediscovered the Church music of Old Russia, nor the boundless wealth of its religious painting, which is the purest, strongest and most original flower of Old Russian civilization."

Nikon won against the Old Believers, but he lost against the nobility, which succeeded in detaching the sympathies of the Tsar from the Patriarch. The same Council which in 1667, in the presence of the Patriarchs of Alexandria and Antioch,

[1] In his introduction to *The Life of the Archpriest Avvakum by Himself* The Hogarth Press, 1924.

excommunicated the Old Believers, deposed Nikon himself and banished him into monastic seclusion.

The line of Patriarchs continued until 1700 when Adrian the last of the original succession died. By this time the dynamic personality of Peter the Great had appeared on the scene and inaugurated a new period in Russian history. In building the city on the Neva which bore his own name he opened his famous "window upon Europe" through which a hurricane blew which disturbed, scattered and rearranged many things in the life of the Russians. Peter admired all things Western and was determined to make Russia a great nation after the pattern of the West. So far as the Russian Church was concerned Peter's reforms had little if any effect in the sphere of doctrine, but he saw to it that bishops were appointed who sympathized or at least were ready to co-operate with his critical ideas on traditional Russian customs and who were willing to acquiesce in the subservience of the ecclesiastical hierarchy to his own autocratic will. Most important of all, he permitted no election of a successor to the Patriarch Adrian, and twenty-one years later abolished the Patriarchate altogether. The formal instrument by which this change was made was entitled the "Ecclesiastical Regulation". There were to be no more Patriarchs in Russia, instead the supreme authority in the Church was to be vested in a body formed on the German Lutheran model and known as the Holy Governing Synod.

This was no synod in the ordinary ecclesiastical sense of the word, but a committee whose members were appointed and dismissed at the will of the Tsar. In addition a secular official called the Procurator was appointed by the Emperor. This layman was not indeed a member of the synod, but his function was to supervise all its proceedings, and without his consent the synod could enact nothing, nor even choose what matters it should discuss. The bishops were dragooned into acceptance of this system, completely foreign as it was to the spirit of the Russian Church. Yet Peter's organization lasted until the collapse of the Empire in 1917.

It is an eloquent testimony to the dynamic force of Peter's personality that the impetus of his reforming movement survived his death. But it introduced deep cleavages and confusion into Russian life. The Court and governing classes in St. Petersburg became the least Russian of all sections of the nation, indeed they were more German than Russian, and for long the reform of Peter affected only the educated classes of society. Behind the St. Petersburg façade was the great mass of the people who continued to regard everything Western with suspicion and even abhorrence. Nevertheless, the movement gradually made headway and in due course the interplay of Western ideas and native Russian thought was to produce modern Russian culture and especially the astonishing achievement of Russian nineteenth-century literature.

The "Westernizers" who believed that the destiny of Russia was to follow the path of the West, and the "Slavophils" who put their faith in the Orthodox tradition of native Russian culture, sharpened their wits upon each other in drawing-room discussions and set forth their views in books. But behind all this and but little affected by it, the religious life of the Russian people went on as before. The official Church and the majority of the hierarchy supported the Government even if they disapproved of things Western. Tsar and Metropolitan needed each other, for each believed that in the preservation of the other his own well-being was involved.

But the schism inherited from the seventeenth century still continued and the "Old Believers", among whom was conserved much that was most profound and sincere in the traditional religion of Russia, would have no truck with the St. Petersburg Empire which was anathema to them, nor with the official Church which had come to terms with it. There were in course of time many groups of these interesting schismatics, some of whom had a clergy and some had not. If sections of them degenerated into sects which were psychologically abnormal, the bulk of them, consolidated by persecution and fanatically tenacious of their beliefs, upheld a high standard of conduct and their communities were a storehouse of many significant and beautiful elements of Russian Orthodoxy. Although after 1800 some availed themselves of more generous terms offered them for reconciliation to the Church, the Old Believers exist to this day as a well-organized body of some millions under their own bishops.

The Old Believers maintain, not without some show of reason, that it is the official Church which has left them, not *vice versa*. But in any case the vast bulk of the Russian people remained within the fold of that official Church. They lived their lives in close contact with their village churches oblivious of the disputes of Slavophils and Westernizers, pathetically constant in their belief in their Little Father, the Orthodox Tsar, and shocked but silent if they heard of time-serving prelates. Nor were men lacking to guide and uphold them. In the eighteenth century Tikhon Zadonsky is an instance of the devout hard-working and conscientious bishop by no means rare in post-Petrine Russia.[1] He stayed at his episcopal post although yearning for the life of secluded devotion for which he had to wait so many years. Some reflection of this man's personality is to be seen in the portrayal of Zossima in Dostoyevsky's *Brothers Karamazov*. In the monasteries were to be found men conspicuous for their sanctity and well qualified to give advice and spiritual help to the many who sought them out. Zossima is not alone in Russian literature and the counterparts of these men in real life, such as St. Serafim of Sarov, Ambrosius of the Monastery of Optina, and many less well-known men of the kind, stand in the true line of descent from Nil Sorsky, in their spirituality and unworldliness and their essentially Russian love of freedom.

The vitality of the Russian Church during the period after Peter and especially in the nineteenth century found expression in widespread missionary activity (see below, p. 162). If the expansion of the Church took place together with the expansion of the Empire, if the missionary bishop worked hand in hand with the secular official and imposed Russian religion and Russian rule at the same time, who is to say which was the dominating motive? At any rate it cannot be said that the Russian Church was blind or indifferent to the spiritual needs of its pagan fellow subjects of the Tsar. But if the State was benevolently interested in the Church, it was determined to control it, and the position of outstanding men like Platon under Katharine II and Paul, and Philaret under Alexander I

[1] Gorodetsky: *The Humiliated Christ in Modern Russian Thought*, pp. 99 ff.

was a difficult one, so long as they held high office. Each of these men was a thinker and theologian of distinction whose writings are regarded as having high authority in the Orthodox Church. Philaret in particular was the author of the celebrated *Confession* which bears his name and the translator into Russian of the Acts of the Synod of Jerusalem, with its important variations from the original (see p. 89). He was interested also in projects for educational and financial reform. But the autocratic action of the sovereign and the paralysing effect of the régime of the Holy Synod with its Procurator made it clear that the State must find more pliable material to fill the highest offices in the Church. Both Platon and Philaret were dismissed to their own dioceses and retired in official disgrace, although each of them continued to exercise great influence through his writing and preaching.

In the summer of 1917, between the March and October Revolutions, the All-Russian Church Council met in Moscow. Its members were both clerical and lay and representative of all classes within the Russian Church. It embarked upon the planning of a wide programme of administrative reform, it swept away Peter's Holy Governing Synod, and restored the Patriarchate of Moscow. Tikhon, Metropolitan of Moscow, whose name was soon to become well-known throughout the world, was appointed by lot from among three elected candidates, to occupy the Patriarchal Throne.

After the triumph of the Bolsheviks and the establishment of the Soviet Government, the world was startled to witness the attempt of a modern Government to suppress religion.[1] No doubt the close association of the Russian Church with the hated Tsarist régime of which it had on occasion shown itself the willing agent, helped to exacerbate the hostility with which the men who had overthrown the Tsar regarded the Church. But it is important to note that their hostility was not directed to this or that bad feature of any particular manifestation of religion, but against religion as such, and, if some of their spokesmen are to be believed, against "good" religion even

---

[1] For a balanced and judicious examination of the whole struggle, see P. B. Anderson : *People's Church and State in Modern Russia*. S.C.M. Press, 1944.

more than "bad". They adopted with enthusiasm the philosophy of Karl Marx and his interpretation of history, and were sincerely convinced that the welfare of mankind necessitated the "liquidation" of religion. No effort was spared and much skill and ingenuity were employed to achieve this end. But though great suffering was caused to individual men and women, and the external organization of the Russian Church was for a time unable to function, and although large numbers of people were induced to abandon at least the outward profession of their faith, yet the lapse of time made it clear that the religion of Russia was not to be eliminated either by physical repression or by argument and propaganda, and that the secular authorities would have to come to terms with it.

The process of finding a *modus vivendi* was greatly facilitated in consequence of the Second German War. When Hitler invaded Russia, the Russian Church unhesitatingly embraced its share in the sufferings of the whole people, gave its blessing to the armies which defended Russian soil and called for national solidarity under the leadership of the Soviet Government in the protection of the Fatherland. In turn the Government decided that it no longer had anything to fear from the Church and was glad to enlist its help in the conduct of the great struggle.

How far, if at all, the new relation of Church and State has been purchased by modification and adjustments of the Church's ideals and standards, time will show. The public utterances of Soviet churchmen today have nothing but thanks and congratulations to offer the secular authority. The Church, they say, is free to live its spiritual life and, what is more, always has been since the October Revolution. The outsider who reads this may be pardoned a suspicion that the lady doth protest too much and that the heroic spiritual power which held its own unbowed before the onslaughts of a foe, has to some extent succumbed to the seductive blandishments of a friend. Yet such a judgment may after all turn out to be unfounded and unfair. If the Russian Church has indeed found a way, with its spiritual integrity unimpaired, to co-operate with an atheist secular authority, not only can it do much if it will to contribute to the sorely needed understanding between Russia and the West, but the fruit it has produced in so much tension and suffering may be such as other parts of the Christian Church may be glad to garner in time of need.

Christianity in Russia has had a very different history from Christianity in Western countries. For long it lived its life in isolation from the West. Its clergy knew no Greek or Latin and the discussions of the Schoolmen passed them by. It had no share in Luther's Reformation or the Counter Reformation and only indirectly felt their effects. It has had, and still has, its own problem of the relation of Church and State and its own ways of dealing with the education and training of its flock. If in modern times it has relied too much upon the external support of the State, it has nevertheless known that its real strength lay in the people's natural sense of religion and the reality of spiritual things.

It is reported that an anti-religious agitator in haranguing a Russian crowd called upon God, if there were one, to strike him dead. When nothing happened he inferred to his hearers that there was no God because He had not killed him. "No," said the crowd, "He hasn't, but we will." And they did. The story, if true, illustrates also the "dionysian" element in the Russian temperament, which is so liable to sweep them into violent action and constitutes one pole in that striking dualism which runs through Russian character.

But there is better evidence of the religious spirit of the Russians in their feeling for God in nature, their sense of beauty as a link with the divine, their admiration, and in spite of all, their practice of the virtues of charity and humility. The ordinary Russian feels that he can hardly be less than charitable and forgiving in view of the shortcomings of all men before God. In spite of his own liability to outbreaks of violence, the idea of administering capital or indeed even corporal punishment in cold blood, sends a chill of revulsion through him.

There is indeed a strand in Russian religion which administers a shock of surprise to the modern Western who derives his impressions of Russia from newspaper accounts of the activities of the Russian State. Long before the Little Poor Man of Assisi changed clothes with the leper and gave his special inspiration to the religious life of the West, the deaths of the princes Boris and Gleb had made an indelible impression upon the religious thought of Russia. In the interpretation put upon their fate by the Russian Church they became the type of voluntary acceptance of suffering. This aspect of their religion which works so powerfully beneath the surface in the thought of Russians, and leads them to look upon suffering, and especially suffering which is voluntarily accepted, not merely with compassion but with veneration, is not to be dismissed as no more than a manifestation of the melancholy inherent in the Slav temperament. It has its reinforcement, if not its foundation, in the Russian stress upon the "kenotic" Christ, the Christ who emptied Himself of His glory and accepted humiliation and suffering to the culminating point of voluntary death. It is this that makes the Russian regard human suffering and humility, not only suffering for Christ but the mere fact of following Christ in His experience of it, with a sort of admiration and reverence.

It is closely associated with the aesthetic approach to religion and with the sense of man's kinship with the natural world. It makes itself felt in the Russian's scale of values in the sphere of law and of ethics and indeed in his general view of life.

As Fedotov points out, of all the iconographic representations of the Virgin and Child which the Russians took over from the Byzantine Church, the type which they call "umilenie" became easily the favourite. It does not so much claim awe before the majestic dignity of the Mother of God, as express that complex emotional reaction of the human heart to innocence and beauty and pain, for which English has no single word.

The "kenoticism" of Russian religion is but one aspect of it, by its very nature it does not claim attention through any violent expression of itself in the world of affairs. But it is an aspect which must not be overlooked.

In Russia, as in the rest of the Orthodox world,[1] the monastic life has always exercised an immense influence. The life of a good monk is regarded as the Christian life *par excel-*

[1] See Chapter X.

ence and his cloister the place where in this world of sin one may meet with God. The great monasteries of Russia, and pre-eminently the Lavra of St. Sergius near Moscow, have been focal points where national aspirations have been gathered up and presented before the mercy of God. Thither multitudes of men and women have flocked with their individual troubles of a burdened conscience or an anxious mind or perhaps simply a hungry body.

The monk may not be a priest, indeed in most cases he is not, but it is to him that the devout will turn for guidance and direction in spiritual matters and to him they unburden their souls. The starets is a characteristic and significant figure in Russian religion. His name means "elder"; he is old in spiritual experience, and distinguished by his piety and gift for guiding other souls. A new member of the monastic community is entrusted to the care of a starets, who trains and teaches him, and devout lay folk living in the world will choose their starets, and resort to him as to a father confessor and director.[1]

[1] For a picture of a typical starets see the writer's translation of *The Way of a Pilgrim*. London, 1931. Another is Father Zossima in Dostoyevsky's novel : *The Brothers Karamazov*.

H

PART II

CHAPTER VIII

ORTHODOX WORSHIP

THE churches in which the Orthodox worship are prevailingly of what is known roughly as the Byzantine type. They are built on the ground plan of a Greek cross, one in which all the four limbs are of equal length. This is squared off by the containing walls beyond which the arms of the cross do not project. The crossing is covered by a dome and the four little squares left in the corners of the big square are often covered by domes also. The domes are raised upon drums, sometimes relatively high ones, which gives a characteristic and decorative appearance to the outside of the building, but with its funnel-like effect perhaps not so successful when seen from within. The square may be prolonged to the east where it ends in three apses covered by half domes, and to the west in a narthex which may be large enough to rival the main church in its proportions. This simple plan lends itself to much variety and elaboration and highly decorative effects are often produced by the multiplication of domes and cupolas and by the use of colour and pattern on the exterior walls.

There are ancient churches of the basilican form still used by Orthodox worshippers, such as the superb Church of the Holy Nativity at Bethlehem, which is said to be the oldest Christian church still in use and is erected over the traditional site of the birth of Christ. It was built by Helena, the mother of Constantine in 326, but restored and enlarged by Justinian in the sixth century.

The Russians took over the Byzantine style of church building, and added characteristic touches of their own, such as the curious onion-shaped cupola so often seen on Russian churches.

Some Orthodox churches are built of ornamental stone, and colour and patterns are introduced in the exterior walls by the use of brick and stone in conjunction. This may be seen particularly in many mediaeval Serbian churches, and in Rumania the churches are often adorned with outside paintings.

But the supreme achievement of Orthodox architecture, if not of all ecclesiastical building, is the Church of the Holy Wisdom, St. Sophia at Constantinople, which the Emperor Justinian began in the year 532 and which was consecrated five years later. The architect achieved the feat of placing a dome less than hemispherical, and with a diameter of 107 feet, upon a square. Later the rim of the dome was raised and pierced by forty windows, the effect produced by the whole being of astonishing lightness and beauty.

In the interior of an Orthodox church there are ordinarily no seats for the congregation; the normal attitude of the Orthodox at worship is standing. Their services are long compared with Western rites, but the congregation stands throughout, including the sermon should there be one. The choir also stands, in a group with their choirmaster. They are usually out of sight and they wear no distinctive robes. The singing, which is often of great beauty, especially among the Russians, is entirely unaccompanied, no instrumental music being allowed in Orthodox worship.

But perhaps the most striking feature of the interior of an Orthodox church to Western eyes is the great screen, called the *conostas*.[1] It stretches across the width of the church, completely shutting off the east-end and hiding the altar from view. It must not be confused with the chancel screen of Western Christendom. Its situation is technically quite different—it occupies the position of the Communion rails in a Western church, and separates not the whole chancel, but the sanctuary, from the rest of the church. An interesting difference in terminology may be noted here. In the Orthodox East, the altar

[1] *Ikonostás* is the Russian and most convenient form of the word. The Greek is *eikonostásion*. The form "ikonostasis", often seen in English, is neither Russian nor Greek.

is the name not of a thing but of a place, i.e., that part of the church in which the altar—in the Western sense—stands. The Eastern name for the altar is the throne. Thus in Orthodox parlance the throne stands in the altar.

Some sort of barrier, fencing off the altar from the rest of the church, dates from very early days, and as time went on it took the form of a row of columns joined by a continuous base and an entablature. The spaces between the columns were filled in with icons, hence the name iconostas, the stand for the icons. It may be constructed of wood or brick or stone or even in rare cases of precious metal. But be it simple or elaborately rich, whether it is in a cathedral or a village church, it will be upon the iconostas that the builders will lavish their resources. It is pierced by three doors, double doors in the centre which when opened disclose the altar and the apse beyond, and single doors at each side. The one to the north opens into what is known as the Chapel of the Prothesis, and the one to the south into the vestry. The iconostas normally reaches from wall to wall, but it is of varying height. It may reach from floor to roof. The development of the iconostas into the great timber erection stretching to the full height of the church is thought to be of Russian origin, the earliest examples of such iconostases are indeed found in and around Novgorod and belong to the fourteenth and fifteenth centuries.

The iconostas is covered with icons, not haphazard but arranged in rough conformity with a general scheme. Thus upon the Royal doors are painted the four Evangelists and the Annunciation, and above them the Last Supper. To the south of the doors is the Icon of Our Lord and next to it the icon of the Patron Saint of that particular church. On the other side of that Royal door is an icon of Our Lady. The centre of the first tier of icons above the doors is occupied by the *Deesis*,[1] a triple icon showing Our Lord enthroned, with Our Lady on His right and St. John the Baptist on His left. This is, so to speak, the heart of the iconostas, the whole assembly of icons being built round it with the faces of the figures turned towards it. It is flanked on either side by the Archangels Gabriel and Michael and the twelve Apostles. The tier next above shows

[1] Prayer.

icons of Feasts of the Church, often of the Twelve Great Festivals of Orthodoxy.[1] In the fourth tier are Old Testament Prophets including King David and King Solomon. Above this may be another row depicting the Patriarchs and perhaps still another filled with Cherubim and Seraphim. The scheme is not rigidly adhered to in detail, but the whole represents all creation, representatives of the Old and the New Covenants grouped in praise and intercession around the Deesis.

To the Orthodox worshipper the iconostas symbolizes the meeting place of heaven and earth: it marks the distinction and at the same time the union, of the world of divine truth and beauty represented by the sanctuary, and this imperfect world of human life symbolized by the rest of the church. As he stands in worship he contemplates this representation of all creation united in a symphony of praise and adoration. And the great doors in the centre of the iconostas mark the place where his worship reaches its climax in the solemn act of Communion. But the whole interior of the church is adorned with images in fresco or mosaic of saints and heroes of the Orthodox Faith. The triumph over iconoclasm was to lead in the eleventh and twelfth centuries to an outburst of elaborate iconography which characterized what used to be known as the "Second Golden Age" of Byzantine art and which made the walls of their churches a picture book in which the Orthodox found a perpetual reminder of their creed. On the walls of the narthex and the nave are depicted the great festivals of the Church, and series of ascetics, confessors, martyrs, doctors and prelates. In the half dome over the apse of the sanctuary is the Theotókos—the God-bearer seated with her Child in her arms, while high up in the great dome this whole iconographic proclamation of belief is crowned by the image of Christ, the rainbow-throned Almighty surrounded by cherubim and seraphim.

Within this building the principal act of worship is the Liturgy, the name which the Orthodox give to the service

[1] These are (not counting Easter, which is in a class by itself) : Christmas, Epiphany, Palm Sunday, Ascension Day, Whit Sunday, Transfiguration, Exaltation of the Holy Cross, and the following feasts of Our Lady: Nativity, Purification, the Annunciation, Presentation in the Temple, and the Falling Asleep.

which elsewhere in Christendom is called the Mass, or the Eucharist, or the Communion Serivce, or the Lord's Supper. There are three Liturgies in use among the Orthodox. The Liturgy of St. Chrysostom is by far the most frequently used and is the normal service. The Liturgy of St. Basil is used on the first five Sundays in Lent, on the Thursday and Saturday before Easter, on Christmas Day and Epiphany if they fall on a Sunday or Monday, otherwise on their eve; and on St. Basil's Day (January 1st).

There is very little difference between the Liturgies of St. Chrysostom and St. Basil; the former is a somewhat shortened form of the latter, the same general structure being maintained.

There is a traditional feeling among the Orthodox that the joyousness of the Liturgy in its complete form is not altogether suitable to the penitential season of Lent, except on Saturdays and Sundays. On Wednesdays and Fridays during that season and on the first three days of Holy Week, therefore, the Liturgy of the Pre-Sanctified is substituted for the ordinary Liturgy. It consists of Vespers and part of the usual Liturgy, the significant omission being the act of Consecration. Those who make their communions at the Liturgy of the Pre-Sanctified do so from the Sacred Elements consecrated on the previous Sunday and reserved for the purpose. This explains the name "pre-sanctified".

The Liturgies are in use in a number of different languages. Among the Greek-speaking peoples the Liturgy is said in Greek; in Russia and among the Slavs of the Balkans—in old Slavonic, and in the several appropriate places the Liturgy will be heard in Georgian, Arabic, Rumanian, Esthonian, Lettish, various Finnish and Tartar dialects, Japanese, Chinese, and even German and English (among Orthodox colonists in North America). The Russian Church has spread the Christian religion to the north and across Siberia to the Far East—and everywhere it has provided for worship in the language of the people.[1]

The form of Christian worship has changed but little in the conservative East as the centuries have passed, and the

[1] See Bolshakoff : *The Foreign Missions of the Russian Orthodox Church* London, 1943.

Liturgy is today practically the same as it was in the sixth century.

The part of the rite called the Prothesis, i.e., the Preparation of the Bread and Wine, has been transferred from the middle of the service to the beginning, where it now forms a complicated and elaborately symbolic introduction to the service. The congregation is not usually present at this first part of the Liturgy, the laity for the most part come in when the Liturgy of the Catechumens[1] begins. The division between the Liturgy of the Catechumens and the Liturgy of the Faithful is still preserved. The Catechumens are prayed for and then dismissed with the cry of the Deacon, "Let all catechumens depart", although it is many centuries since this had any practical significance. The Deacon still calls "The Doors, the Doors" that they may be guarded before the recitation of the Creed and the entrance upon the most solemn part of the rite.

After a few attendances at the Orthodox Liturgy those who are accustomed to the Roman Catholic or Church of England rites will soon learn to recognize the same general structure of the service in East and West alike, though the framework is filled out at much greater length in the East.

The outstanding feature of the Liturgy of the Catechumens is the reading of the Epistle and Gospel, preceded by the Little Entrance.[2] They are embodied in a setting of Psalms, Canticles and Litanies, the last being recited by the Deacon as he stands outside the Royal doors and facing East.

In the Liturgy of the Faithful we note the familiar sequence of Offertory, Creed (in that order in the East), *Sursum Corda* ("Lift up your hearts"—"We lift them up unto the Lord"), *Sanctus* ("Holy, Holy, Holy") and Consecration. But in addition to the large number of variable parts of the service in Orthodox worship and all the rich embellishment of Canticle and Anthem, there is also a difference in relative external

[1] Those undergoing instruction preparatory to Baptism. Beside being the name of the whole rite, the word Liturgy is also applied to each of two divisions of it known as the Liturgy of the Catechumens and the Liturgy of the Faithful.

[2] i.e., the entry of the clergy from the Chapel of the Prothesis, with the Book of the Gospels. It is "little" as compared with the "Great Entrance" later in the Service.

emphasis, in dramatic stress. Thus in the West everything plainly leads up to the Consecration as the climax of the rite not only in its inner meaning but in its outward aspect. In the Orthodox Liturgy, however, the Consecration might even escape the notice of one who was not accustomed to follow the rite or attentive to note it. The Consecration is, of course, actually its climax in East and West alike, but in the East no special outward signs of it are visible to the congregation, the Royal doors which shut off the Sanctuary being closed.

On the other hand the Great Entrance is easily the most conspicuous part of the whole service. It corresponds to the offertory in the West, i.e., the bringing of the bread and wine to be offered at the altar. In the West this is the simplest of actions[1] and involves no more than moving the bread and wine a few feet from a small table called the Credence, to the Altar. In the East it is the occasion of a solemn procession in which all the clergy present and their attendants pass out through the northern door of the iconostas, along the front of it, and after a pause for biddings to prayer, in again through the Royal doors. All this is done with pomp and circumstance, the choir meanwhile singing the Cherubic hymn.

The deportment of the worshippers is to be noted. They take little audible part in the service—there are no hymns in the Western sense—but they often join in the Lord's Prayer aloud and sometimes in the Creed. They cross themselves frequently (making the sign from right to left) and kneel or even prostrate themselves as devotion moves them. There is much freedom and spontaneity of action. Men, women and children are all gathered together in the nave, occupying any particular part in it which takes their fancy. They move about from one place to another if they are so disposed and go up to salute an icon or place a lighted candle whenever they are moved to do so. It is quite unlike an English congregation, in which all do the same thing at the same time. The Orthodox habit is more free and easy. But at the same time it is less so, for the Orthodox stands to worship, and this not simply in the sense of not sitting or not kneeling. It is more like standing

---

[1] But compare the Offertory as performed in Westminster Abbey and some other Anglican churches.

o attention. If he is well brought up in this respect the Orthodox worshipper will stand erect with his feet together, his hands by his side, with head up and eyes looking straight before him o the east end of the church. His bodily posture expresses, and perhaps contributes to, the active share he is taking in what is going on. Ideally he is rendering praise and glory to God for all that He is and does, and at the same time he is presenting himself before God and submitting himself to the divine scrutiny.

At the time of Communion, the celebrant and other officiating clergy make their communion in both kinds, separately, as in the West. The priest and deacon then come out through the Royal doors and stand just outside them. The priest holds the chalice, into which the consecrated breads have been put. Lay communicants then approach and are given their communion standing, in both kinds, but administered together by means of a spoon placed between the communicant's lips. He then wipes his lips on a silk napkin which hangs over the deacon's arm, takes a sip of water and a small piece of bread (not, of course, consecrated) from a table standing near and returns to the body of the church.

The words of administration are "The servant of God, N——, receives the precious and holy Body and Blood of Jesus Christ, unto remission of sins and unto everlasting life", to children "unto everlasting life" only).

At the end of the service all present go up to the Royal gates and in turn kiss a cross held out to them by the priest: and small pieces of bread which have been blessed are distributed and eaten.

The Orthodox rite is, generally speaking, a good deal longer than the Western, though not so much so as appears from the printed page. For at certain times the priest's part and the deacon's are going on simultaneously—the deacon being outside the iconostas and leading the devotions of the people in a litany, while the priest is saying the prayers allotted to him within the Sanctuary. Still, Orthodox services are sometimes of great length, the Russians in particular having long been notorious in this respect, though modern times have brought some concessions to human frailty. "God grant us His special aid to get through the whole of this present week. As for the Muscovites their feet must surely be of iron"—was the pathetic lament of the Archdeacon of Aleppo who was in Moscow for Holy Week and Easter in the year 1656. He complained bitterly of services which lasted from "early dawn" until "the eleventh hour".[1]

The Orthodox Liturgy has been frequently described. The Daily Offices of the Orthodox Church, however, i.e., it regular liturgical services other than the Liturgy, are perhaps not so familiar, and the structure and shape of the service are not so easy to grasp. Even with a translation before him the reader is daunted by a bewildering variety of rubrics and sub titles of portions of the service. Certain details strike him at once as curious. The *Magnificat* is a morning canticle, for instance, and the *Te Deum* does not appear at all in the regular sequence of liturgical services. The *Gloria in excelsis* is said at Mattins and at Compline, and the Nicene Creed at the midnight service and Compline. There is also a richness, variety and flexibility about the Orthodox offices in the highest degree contrasted with the sober regularity of our own.

Theoretically the daily offices—Vespers, Compline, the midnight service, Mattins, Prime, Terce, Sext and None—are spread out over the twenty-four hours to form one unbroken offering of prayer and praise. In practice, however, they are, at least in parish churches, grouped together. The recitation of None, Vespers and Compline constitutes the evening service the midnight service, Mattins and Prime are said together at the morning service, while Terce and Sext are combined with the Liturgy at some convenient hour, perhaps about ten o'clock in the morning. This grouping of the offices may vary somewhat on Sundays and the great festivals, when the all night vigil service, consisting of Vespers, Mattins and Prime is recited at about six o'clock on the evening before. In monasteries where everything is sung in full, and slowly, this service

---

[1] *The Travels of Macarius*, p. 46.
[2] For the text see : *Brightman Liturgies Eastern and Western*, Oxford 1896.

The Russian novelist Gogol wrote a mystical commentary on the Liturgy which has been translated into English : *Meditations on the Divine Liturgy* London, 1926.

ay last literally all night, but as used in parish churches it
kes about two hours.

In common with the rest of Christendom the Orthodox
nurch uses the Psalter and lections from the rest of Holy
ripture in the structure of its services. But the characteristic
ature of Orthodoxy in this regard is its inclusion of a very
rge element of religious poetry. Something more will be said
out this later on.

Two of the many books required by the officiant are known
the "Apostle" and the "Gospel". The four Gospels are
cluded in the latter, while the former contains the Acts of
e Apostles as well as the Epistles. The Epistle and Gospel
the day are read at the Liturgy according to a fixed order,
d the Gospel is read at Mattins also. In addition to the
rmal division into chapters and verses the books are also
rtioned out into sections and the order in which these sections
e to be used is given at the end of the books. For each day in
ch week of the year, beginning at Easter, the proper section
shown, and there are special lections provided for the greater
stivals and for the Occasional Offices.

The Psalter is used in three ways. First, each of the offices
s its own fixed psalms to be recited daily. In addition to this
e whole Psalter is divided into twenty sections called
athismata, and each Kathisma again into three Staseis. The
loria is said at the end of each Stasis, not at the end of each
salm. Thus arranged the Psalter is used at Mattins and
espers, in addition to their fixed psalms. In Lent all twenty
athismata are read through twice in each week. From Maundy
hursday till Low Sunday they are omitted altogether. But
uring the rest of the year two Kathismata are said at Mattins
d one at Vespers and thus the recitation of the Psalter is
ore or less completed in one week. The third manner in which
e Psalter is used is by the incorporation into the service of
etached verses from the psalms, singly or in groups. For
xample, two verses (hardly ever consecutive) of a psalm are
id before the Epistle in the Liturgy, and repeated in the
ffices. They are called the prokeimenon of the day.

Such then roughly is the use of the psalms and lessons.
he actual prayers in the narrower sense of the word, which

are used in the office, are many of them very beautiful. The
are often long and couched in poetic phraseology, quite differer
in form from the concise and regular Western Collect. Fr
quently they are said silently by the priest while the cho
are singing their part. Thus while the reader reads the si
psalms at Mattins, the priest recites the twelve mornin
prayers, the first three within the Altar (i.e., in Wester
phraseology, the Sanctuary), and the remainder outside th
iconostas, facing the Royal doors. The same is true of th
Seven Prayers of Light at Vespers. The following, which i
said at all the hours, may be given as an example:

"O thou who at all times and seasons in heaven an
earth art worshipped and glorified, Christ our God, long
suffering, pitiful and all-compassionate, who lovest th
righteous and pitiest sinners, who callest all to salvatio
through the gospel of thy coming kingdom, do thou, (
Lord, receive our prayers at this time, and guide our live
in thy statutes. Sanctify our souls, cleanse our bodies
correct our thoughts, purify our hearts, and deliver us fron
all affliction, evil and pain. Defend us by thy holy angels
that, being guarded and guided by their ranks, we ma
come to the unity of the faith and the knowledge of thin
unapproachable glory, who art blessed to ages of ages
Amen."

But the bulk of the Orthodox services consist of ecclesiastica
poetry. It has been computed that poetry comprises 80 per cen
of the vast contents of the service books, and it is made up fo
the most part of short hymns. The word "hymn" is not her
used in the modern and Western sense with its implication o
metre and perhaps rhyme. They are rhythmical composition
in poetical language—hymns in the sense that the *Gloria i
excelsis* may be so called. A general name which covers a larg
number of them is *troparion* (Slavonic: *tropar*), and the Ortho
dox services are festooned with them, strung together with
Glorias and broken verses from the psalms like pearls on
string. The number of different sorts of *troparia* is large an
the total of all sorts must run into many thousands. The deacor
Romanus, who lived about A.D. 500, is credited with th

omposition of over a thousand *kontakia*. A *kontakion* is one
f those short "hymns" summing up the life of a saint or
iving the gist of the occasion for which it is used. This is the
ontakion of Easter Day:

> "Thou, O Immortal, thou didst descend into the tomb,
> yet didst thou overthrow the might of Hades, O Christ
> our God; and thou didst arise as Victor, saying to the
> Ointment-bearers—Hail! Thou didst give peace to thine
> Apostles, who dost cause them that are fallen to arise."

A *Theotókion* is a hymn about or addressed to Our Lady:

> "Formed wert thou to be the dwelling of light, pure
> and most holy Mother and Virgin, who didst give birth to
> Christ the King of all and the Enlightener of them that sit
> in darkness: whence with faith we bless thee."

A *Stavro-theotókion* is the same, but contains also a refer-
nce to the Cross:

> "Standing by the Cross of thy Son and the Son of God,
> and beholding his long-suffering, with tears, pure Mother,
> thou saidst, Woe is me! Why sufferest thou thus unjustly,
> my Son, Word of God, for the race of men?"

These must suffice as illustrations of the three or four dozen
ifferent varieties of *troparia*. Many of them are of great
eauty. A few have been translated, put into modern dress,
nd become favourites in our hymn books. Thus the original
f "Hail, gladdening Light" is the *troparion* which occupies in
he Orthodox Vespers the position which *Magnificat* holds in
he West.

> "Joyful Light of the holy glory of the Father, Immortal,
> Heavenly, Holy, Blessed O Jesu Christ; we, having come
> to the setting of the sun and beholding the evening light,
> hymn God, Father, Son and Holy Ghost. It is meet at all
> times that thou shouldst be hymned with auspicious voices,
> Son of God, Giver of Life: wherefore the world glorifieth
> thee."

t has been sung at Vespers at least since the time of St. Basil.

who ascribes it to the martyr Athenogenes, about A.D. 17
"The day is past and over", "Stars of the morning", "Th
Day of Resurrection", "Come, ye faithful, raise the strain
"Fierce raged the tempest", and others are all examples
modern renderings of Orthodox *troparia*.

The *troparia* have been likened to pearls on a string. On
might also think of them as pieces of mosaic fitted togethe
into an intricate pattern which can itself be picked up as
whole and placed here or there as required. Such is that ver
important element in Orthodox worship known as a *Kanor*
some rough and generalized description of which is necessar
in even this brief survey. There are *kanons* of the great festival
most Saints' days have their *kanons*, and some have more tha
one, and there are *kanons* in some of the Occasional Offices
One of the best known composers of *kanons* is St. Joh
Damascene, another is Anatolius, Patriarch of Constantinopl
in the fifth century, and many *kanons* are of great antiquity
Their structure is as follows: three, four, five or more *tropari*
(the number varies) form an *ode*, and nine *odes* make a *kanon*
But in addition to their own subject-matter the *odes* ar
supposed to conform to, or contain some allusion to, certai
scriptural prototypes.
These are:—

(1) The Song of Israel (Exod. xv, 1–21).
(2) The Song of Moses (Deut. xxxii, 1–44).
(3) The Song of Hannah (1 Sam. ii, 1–11).
(4) The Prayer of Habakkuk (iii, 1–19).
(5) The Prayer of Isaiah (xxvi, 9–21).
(6) The Prayer of Jonah (ii, 2–10).
(7) The Prayer of the Three Children (from the Apocrypha
addition to the third chapter of the Book of Daniel).
(8) The *Benedicite*.
(9) The *Magnificat* and *Benedictus*.

These scriptural *odes* are taken as covering the whole field
of religious emotional experience, and whatever be the occasion
for which the *kanon* is written, its *odes* are skilfully constructed
to carry the mind back to the corresponding scriptural *ode*
Further, each *ode* begins with a verse called a *heirmos*, setting

he rhythmic scheme for the following verses, and ends with a *theotokion* (see above). Various other sorts of *troparia* are inserted at fixed places as the *kanon* progresses, and after *Ode* 6 there may be a whole group of them, beginning with a *kontakion*; and even a litany and a lection.

The *Ectine* or Litany is another element which enters freely into the composition of Orthodox services. There are four forms of Litany used both in the Liturgy and the offices: the Great Litany, the Little Litany, the Increased Litany (so called from its triple response) and the Petitioning Litany. To these may be added the Litany of the Catechumens which belongs to the Liturgy alone, and the Litany of the Faithful Departed which is said on occasion at the Liturgy, and in the Office of the Dead. The Litanies are said by the deacon standing before the Royal gates. He holds the end of his stole in his right hand and crosses himself with it before he bows at the end of each petition. The Litany ends with an "exclamation" by the priest, which is the concluding phrases of the prayer which he has been saying secretly during the singing of the Litany. As an example the Petitioning Litany is here given (from King's translation of Vespers):

Deacon: Let us compleat our evening supplication to the Lord.
Choir: Lord, have mercy upon us.
Deacon: Protect us, save us, be merciful unto us, and preserve us by thy grace, O God.
Choir: Lord, have mercy upon us.
Deacon: Let us beseech the Lord that we may finish this evening in holiness, peace, and innocence.
Choir: Grant this, O Lord.
Deacon: Let us beseech the Lord for the angel of peace, the faithful guide and keeper of our souls and bodies.
Choir: Grant this, O Lord.
Deacon: Let us beseech the Lord for pardon and remission of our sins and offences.
Choir: Grant this, O Lord.
Deacon: Let us beseech the Lord for all things good and profitable for our souls and for the peace of the world.
Choir: Grant this, O Lord.

Deacon: Let us beseech the Lord that we may end the rest of our days in peace and repentance.

Choir: Grant this, O Lord.

Deacon: Let us beseech the Lord that the last period of our lives may be suitable to our Christian profession, without pain and confusion of face, that we may give a good answer at the dreadful tribunal of Christ.

Choir: Grant this, O Lord.

Deacon: In remembrance of our most holy, most pure, most blessed and glorious Lady, the Mother of God, and ever-virgin Mary, with all Saints, we commend ourselves and each other, and our whole life to Christ our God.

Choir: To thee, O Lord.

Exclamation

Priest: For thou art the blessed God, the Lover of mankind, and to thee, the Father, the Son and the Holy Ghost, we offer our praise, now and for ever, even unto ages of ages.

Choir: Amen.

The *Trisagion* has its place at the beginning of the Daily Offices and of many other services also. In its extended form it runs as follows:

O Holy God, O Holy Mighty, O Holy Immortal, have mercy upon us (*thrice*).

Glory be to the Father, and to the Son, and to the Holy Ghost, both now and for ever, even unto ages of ages. Amen.

O Most Holy Trinity, have mercy upon us; O Lord, purify us from our sins, and forgive us our transgressions, O Lord: O Holy, look down upon us, and heal our infirmities for thy Name's sake.

Lord, have mercy upon us (*thrice*), and this is followed by the *Gloria* again, and the Lord's Prayer.[1]

One sound will be heard echoing insistently throughout

---

[1] For further details about the Daily Offices and a description of the Occasional Offices of the Orthodox Church, reference may be made to the writer's article in *Liturgy and Worship* (S.P.C.K., 1932), upon which most of the foregoing is based.

Orthodox worship, and that is the praise of the Mother of God. The poetic language of the "hymns", the discursiveness of the phraseology and the repetitions alike lend themselves to the expressing of a devotion which seems, at times, to have no bounds. The *Theotókos*, the God-bearer in her purity, her humility and the glory of her destiny is a theme of which Orthodox worship never tires. Thought and language are ransacked to add to the profusion of epithets and titles of honour which are showered upon her to stress the faith of the Orthodox in the basic truth of Christianity, the Incarnation of the Son of God. It reaches its climax in the Akathist Hymn[1] which is sung either in part or wholly once a week during the first five weeks of Lent. It is the most celebrated poetic achievement of the Byzantine Church and was traditionally attributed to the Patriarch Sergius, who was said to have composed it in thanksgiving for the miraculous deliverance of the City in A.D. 626 (see p. 41) by the protective action of Our Lady. The attribution may not be able to bear the searchlight of historical criticism, but that matters little. The Akathist hymn still expresses at its highest that disinterested and exuberant praise of her who gave human birth to the child Who was God, which from early times has been woven into the very texture of Orthodox worship.

[1] An English translation was published by the St. Dominic Press in 1934.

I

CHAPTER IX

THE ICONS

ALLUSION has been made more than once in this book to the icons; but such is their importance in Orthodox piety that it may be well to devote a short chapter to them.

An icon is a picture of a sacred subject painted upon a panel of wood of varying size. The surface is prepared with a mixture of powdered alabaster and glue beneath which linen is sometimes stretched, and the colours laid on with the yolk of egg as a medium.[1] The finished panel was in many cases furnished later on with a covering of metal, precious or base, which completely hides the painting, except the flesh parts, to reveal which holes were cut in the metal. The rest of the picture, or at least its main lines, are reproduced in the metal cover by *répoussée*. Further embellishment may be added, in the form of haloes and different kinds of pendants. The icon may be adorned with precious stones, some famous examples being encrusted with a wealth of them.

It has been generally accepted that the icon is derived from the funerary portraits of the dead which were placed upon mummies in Egypt.[2] Perhaps by way of usage in connection with the martyrs, and devotion to their shrines, the use of icons spread in time throughout the Orthodox world and became a characteristic feature of Orthodox piety.

The painting of icons was a work of religion as well as a work of art, the painter preparing himself for his task by prayer and other spiritual exercises. In modern times the provision of vast numbers of cheap icons may have degener-

[1] For details in the technique of icon-painting see Minns-Kondakov : *The Russian Icon*, Oxford, 1927.
[2] See, however, A. Frolow : *Revue des Études Byzantines*, Tome VI, 1948, p. 125.

ated into a mere trade, but ideally, and to a large extent in actual fact, the production of them has been and still is the pious activity of monks. The monasteries were the great workshops in which icons were produced, and although icons are nearly always anonymous, the known painters of these highly venerated objects were themselves greatly revered.

The subjects depicted on the icon are many and various. It may be a single figure; of Christ, the Virgin Mary, St. John the Baptist (winged, as the Precursor), or some other saint. It may be a group of figures, a picture of a scriptural or ecclesiastical incident, or the representation of an abstruse theological idea. Miracles, Martyrdoms, Councils of the Church, are drawn by the icon-painter's brush. An icon may even represent the veneration of another icon by some eminent prelate.

The icon-painter did not profess, with possibly some very rare exceptions, to be making a portrait, though the general aspect of a saint will be the same on every icon of him. Nor, in the great days of icon-painting, was realistic truth to nature conceived as an aim. The painter did not produce the illusion of depth, perspective was often reversed, and the niceties of anatomical knowledge ignored. Realism came in with the decadence of the art of icon-painting.

The men who made the icons in the great days of Byzantium and at the zenith of Russian icon-painting in fifteenth-century Novgorod were doing two things. They were decorating a flat surface and they were seeking to convey in line and colour an aspect of divine truth. At their best they achieved both those purposes supremely well.

They painted within the framework of rules about the way that this or that person should be represented, which belonged to the very core of the tradition of icon-painting. Such rules, often concerned with a surprising degree of detail, were embodied in manuals of instruction which circulated among the workshops.

Hence the immediate impression that the numberless icons of any particular subject are "all alike". But it is possible to exaggerate this similarity and to over-rate the influence of the manuals. The great examples of icon-painting reveal the fact that the rules left room for the expression of individual inspiration and the exercise of creative power, as the painter set about his task of adorning a given surface with a vision of divine truth.

As the icons vary in their subject matter, so they vary also in their artistic merit. Some are supreme works of art, many are of great beauty, superb in their composition, rhythm of line and glowing colour. Many others have little aesthetic value, and the icon may even degenerate into a cheap oleograph stuck on a piece of wood.

But the veneration in which they are held is independent of these considerations. Some measure of it may be found in the ubiquity of icons in an Orthodox country. They are not only in churches, but also in public buildings of all kinds, in private houses and shops. There is a recognized position for the icon in a room, and the visitor will salute it on entering, just as he greets his host. Schools, regiments, clubs and the like will adopt their own icons. The devout will carry an icon with them when they travel, and have it before them when they say their prayers. Well-to-do people may accumulate their family icons from generation to generation. The first thing the Orthodox worshipper does on entering his church is to salute the icons, or, at least, such of them as may claim his particular devotion. He bows before them, crosses himself, says a prayer, kisses the icon, and perhaps sets a lighted candle before it in the stand provided for the purpose. He then moves away to wherever he wishes to stand for the service if there is one, or to leave the church and go about his business.

Plainly we are here in a realm which readily lends itself to capture by popular religion. Popular religion, whatever the field in which it expresses itself, the use of the Bible, the singing of subjective and emotional hymns, the veneration of icons, or anything else, may easily use the thing it has captured, in a way which others call superstition, and which may indeed be such.

But before the Westerner draws hasty general conclusions about the Orthodox practice before the icons, he should reflect that the Orthodox approaches the icon with premises in his mind which he himself probably does not share.

It is not a simple matter for a Westerner to grasp what the icon means to the Orthodox and the part it plays in his religious life. Perhaps it can be fully understood only from within Orthodoxy as part of Orthodox experience. But certain distinctions can be drawn. All Christians presumably agree that a picture of a sacred person or event has value and legitimate use as a means of teaching. But the icon is more than that. It is more also than a picture of a loved person, by looking upon which memory is refreshed and devotion stimulated. Neither of these parallels would account for the degree of veneration which is paid to the icons. It is the same veneration as the Orthodox pay to the Book of the Gospels and the Cross. On the other hand it is a lower degree of veneration than that which is given to the consecrated elements of the Eucharist. In the latter case worship is rendered to Christ Himself actually present. In an icon of Christ, He is not conceived as present in the same way as that. Yet there is a link between the actual material icon, and the person it represents. In the devout contemplation of an icon one is brought in some sense into the presence of the original of which it is a painting. The link is in the Orthodox view analogous to the connection between a sacred relic and the saint from which the relic is derived. With this difference, that the connection between the relic and the saint, assuming it to exist in fact, might be called a natural link, whereas the connection between the icon and its original is created by the Church. It is established by the action of blessing the icon. An icon is not, so to speak, fully an icon until it has been blessed. Then it becomes a link between the human and the divine, through it the other world comes into touch with the worshipper.

Standing before it with the right disposition of heart and mind, one is really in touch with, in the presence of, the subject which the icon represents. "According to Orthodox belief an icon is a place of the Gracious Presence. It is the place of an *appearance* of Christ, of the Virgin, of the saints, of all those represented by the icon, and hence it serves as a place for prayer to them." "By the blessing of the icon of Christ, a mystical meeting of the faithful and Christ is made possible."[1]

[1] S. Bulgakov: *The Orthodox Church*, p. 162 f., London, 1935.

No wonder then that the icons are so highly revered, that famous icons are carried in procession through the streets, or brought by the clergy to the bedside of the sick.

So potent is the link between the icon and its prototype that many icons are regarded as "wonder-working icons". In fact the wonder-working icon is the icon *par excellence*. The belief that such icons are endowed with miraculous power has given rise to numberless legends.[1] They may tell of an icon's being the means of curing sickness and other ills which flesh is heir to, of bringing material good fortune to the devout believer, of securing the icon's own safety when menaced by danger, of rewarding its veneration and even resenting and punishing insult, physical injury and neglect, but mercifully restoring the sinner after his repentance. Not all of this is official Orthodox teaching: much of it belongs to the sphere of popular religion, where it may go to fantastic lengths.[2]

Presumably the orthodox interpretation of such happenings is that at the intercession of the saint depicted on the icon, God grants the request of the petitioner who prayed before it. In the popular mind such an explanation may readily slide into the conception that the saint is the benefactor because this particular picture of him was venerated, and that again may easily slip into the feeling that it is the actual icon itself which has worked the miracle or conferred the blessing.

There exist a relatively large number of pictures of the Blessed Virgin which tradition attributes to St. Luke, and these are treated with deep reverence. But a place of their own in the heart of the Orthodox believer belongs to the "Icons not made with Hands". These are icons the originals of which are believed to have come into existence without human agency. Such are the Vernicle, the legend of which is well known in the West also; and an image of Christ imprinted upon a cloth sent to Abgar, King of Edessa, by Christ himself and subsequently brought to Constantinople. This is the most ancient of the "Icons not made with Hands". But there are others, and they, and the copies made of them (though some are said

[1] See R. M. Dawkins for many such connected with the icons of Athos, in *The Monks of Athos*, London, 1936.
[2] Charles Diehl in *Cambridge Mediæval History*, Vol. IV, p. 6.

to be impossible to copy, or even to photograph) are regarded
with the deepest veneration.[1]

The canonical authority upon which the veneration of
icons rests is the decree of the second council of Nicaea which
is the seventh Ecumenical Council (see p. 54). The doctrinal
basis is found in the fact of the Incarnation. God cannot be
represented in His eternal being.[2] But God became man and
took a body of material flesh. Because of this a picture may
lawfully be made of Him. Further, in assuming a human body
He used matter as the vehicle of spirit, rescued it from
corruption and consecrated it to a share in His redemptive
purpose. What is true of Christ's material body, is true of
other forms of matter such as the material elements in the
sacraments, and, in some measure, of the icons. The icons
are, therefore, worthy of veneration, though in theory the
degree of veneration is strictly limited.

[1] R. M. Dawkins has a chapter on "Icons not made with Hands"—in
his *Monks of Athos*, Chapter 18.
[2] Yet icons exist which depict the Holy Trinity as two throned Figures
side by side, with the Dove above them.

CHAPTER X

ORTHODOX MONASTICISM

MONASTICISM is an immensely important institution in the
life of the Orthodox Church. The impulse to flee the world,
to escape from the evil in it and avoid its temptations and to save
one's soul by withdrawal into a life of prayer and contemplation,
has operated upon men and women from almost the earliest
Christian centuries. Already in the third century St. Paul of
Thebes and St. Anthony retired into the Egyptian desert to live
solitary lives as hermits, and many followed their examples.

The attention is caught by the spectacular austerities of
these desert hermits. Their ruthless and ferocious handling
of the flesh often took forms which were gruesome and fantastic to the borders of the incredible. Yet it would be scant
justice to those men to focus attention upon this aspect of their
achievement only. Anthony was the friend of Athanasius, and
men like Athanasius were not unaware of the claims of the
world of human beings upon the Christian believer. Yet the
hermits were regarded with immense veneration and men
flocked to sit at their feet and even to imitate their manner of
life. It was not the mere maceration of the body, nor only the
fear of the world and a selfish desire to save their own souls,
which drew them there. In spite of the extreme and manifold
negations, the fundamental aspiration was positive. The
first dynamic outburst of enthusiasm which led people to sell
their possessions and lay the money at the Apostles' feet,
flared up again in this violent gesture of throwing away everything for the sake of God. The significant thing about these
desert saints was not this or that physical achievement in the
sphere of fasting and self mortification, but their complete
abandon, their wild enthusiasm for God.

Men were awed indeed by the hermit's austerities, but they took note of the fact that the almost inhuman means he chose for his approach to God was answered by something human and lovable in him after all. They saw him as one who in the silence of the desert solitude, famished and sleepless, had looked upon things eternal, and so learned to be humble, while his harshness to himself had its counterpart in his gentleness to other men.

At the beginning of the next century a development took place when St. Anthony during the latter part of his life appears as the head and centre of a group of such solitaries. They were distinct from simple hermits, for they lived as a colony, but there was at this stage no Rule and no formal Vows. Each practised the life of a monk in the way that seemed best to him: he received some guidance from the head of the group, but he was not bound to obey him. A large and increasing number of monks lived this sort of life in the Egyptian desert from the fourth century onwards. But at the same time a further development was taking place, and about the year 320 St. Pachomius founded the first monastery in the true sense of the word, in which the brethren lived a life in common. These monks were subject to a Rule which controlled every aspect of their lives, and owed obedience to their superior. Even in Pachomius' lifetime there existed nine such communities for men and two for women.

The movement increased rapidly and soon there were very large numbers of monks in Egypt, while the eager drive to embrace the monastic life extended northward into Palestine. Here too, fostered by the growing veneration for the Holy Places, many monasteries were founded in the Judaean desert. St. Sabbas was a famous Palestinian monk who himself founded a number of religious houses of the type known as "laura", i.e., consisting of a number of hermits living in separate cells, but under the direction of an abbot. Further north still, in Syria and Mesopotamia the monastic life was developed upon lines which were characterized by extreme austerities outstripping even those of the Egyptian desert. It was in Syria that the pillar-saints first made their appearance, the most famous of them being St. Simeon Stylites who spent thirty years of his life on the top of a pillar, the height of which he gradually

increased from six feet to sixty. He never descended; his dis
ciples supplied him with the necessities of life by means of a
ladder, and his influence upon all classes of society was wide
spread and very great.[1]

But most of these centres were soon to find themselves cu
off from the Orthodox world by the doctrinal controversie
in which the Patriarchates of Alexandria and Antioch wer
involved, and by the invasion of the Arabs. It was throug
Cappadocia that the stream of development in Orthodo
monasticism flowed from its source in Pachomius, and w
reach a definite turning point in the story when the impressiv
figure of St. Basil, later to be Bishop of Caesarea in Pontus
enters upon the scene. He was born in 329 and died in A.D
379, an aristocrat by birth, a man of brilliant intellectual gifts and
of immense prestige. In his own country the monastic life already
existed and he was strongly drawn to it. About the year 35
he made a tour of Syria, Palestine, Egypt and Mesopotamia
to visit the great ascetics and study their manner of life.

He found, therefore, the three types just described, the
Solitary or Eremite, the Antonian or Semi-eremite, and the
Pachomian or Cœnobitic, and it was the last which appealed
to him most powerfully, and which in a modified form he
adopted. His adaptations were chiefly concerned with an
increased emphasis upon the sense of community. "St. Basi
established a common roof, a common table, and commor
prayer always."[2] He also kept the numbers of monks in eac
monastery smaller than was customary in Egypt. With the
weight of his personal ascendancy and of his many writing
on the subject behind it, the Basilian form of monastic life
became prevalent in the Orthodox world.

But the Eremite and the Semi-eremite did not disappear
they have continued to exist to the present day. In fact it i
characteristic of Orthodox monasticism that it may combine
all three forms of the monastic life. This practice was established as early as the end of the fifth century in Palestine and wa
introduced into Mount Athos by a certain St. Athanasius in the

[1] See the life of a pillar saint in Baynes and Dawes, *Three Byzantin
Saints*, Oxford, 1948.
[2] *Camb. Med. Hist.*, I, p. 528.

iddle of the tenth. The general method has been to allow monks
 adopt the life of solitude or semi-solitude only if they felt so
lled, after long experience and training in the common life.

It was not until the last quarter of the fourth century, in
ie reign of Theodosius the Great, that the monastic life
stablished itself on a permanent footing in Constantinople
self. But after that time it developed rapidly and a century
nd a half later, in the capital city and Chalcedon, which was just
cross the water, together there were over a hundred religious
ouses.[1] Councils of the Church, and notably Chalcedon in
51, found it expedient to issue regulations to control the lives
f the monks, defining their duties and placing them under the
upervision of the bishop.

By the time of Justinian, the civil power has taken cog-
izance of the monastic life and the later legislation of that
mperor deals with it in considerable detail. In his *Novels*,
ie ecclesiastical regulations which dealt with monasticism are
onfirmed by the law of the State.

The rules laid down by Justinian, based as they were upon the
ystem of St Basil were wise and beneficial, and well calculated
 stimulate the best in the monastic way of life as well as to safe-
uard it against obvious dangers. Both Church and State re-
iained content with them in the main for a long time to come.
Jnder them monasticism flourished exceedingly, and more and
iore religious houses were founded, both for men and for women.

As monasteries multiplied and increased in size throughout
ie Empire, the need for a more complex organization with
ifferentiation of function within the community became
pparent and even imperative. Few men can be found able to
ike sole responsibility for all the details of every aspect of the
fe of a religious community, and the reforms introduced by
t. Theodore of the monastery of Studius in the ninth century
rought much relief to the lot of an abbot. St. Theodore,
riter, administrator and a fighter, left his mark upon Orthodox
ionasticism in more ways than one. He retired from the world
t an early age and joined a community of which his uncle,
t. Plato, was the superior on a family estate on Mount
)lympus. In due course he succeeded his uncle as superior

[1] Baynes and Moss, *Byzantium*, p. 145.

and later returned, with his monks, to Constantinople, the city of his birth and upbringing. Here he established his community in the derelict buildings of a monastery which had been founded by one named Studius some four centuries earlier This was to become the celebrated Studite Monastery, from which St. Theodore takes his title and which played so important a part in the ecclesiastical politics of Constantinople.

While keeping the central control in the hands of the abbot St. Theodore divided the task of running the monastery among a number of functionaries each of whom had his clearly defined duties and rendered an account of his department periodically to the abbot. St. Theodore assembled his monks three times a week for instruction and exhortation and established a system of discipline within the community Under his rule the monastery of Studius prospered to such an extent that before long there were no less than a thousand monks within its walls.

Monasticism has exercised an immense influence in Orthodoxy; and behind the monks were the people. For in popular estimation the monastic life was the highest expression of Christian discipleship. The veneration which in days of persecution was paid to the martyr was, in a sense, transferred to the spiritual athlete who for the salvation of his soul and the attainment of communion with God devoted himself to prayer and contemplation, and not merely forsook the pleasures of the world, but surrendered everything that could be surrendered while keeping life in the body.

The forms of public worship in the Orthodox Church were compiled by and for the monks. There is no concession in the form of a simplified version for popular use by the laity. The bishops are invariably chosen from the ranks of the monks.

The reputation for sanctity ascribed to the monk as such and frequently deservedly, led men and women of all classes of society to resort to them for spiritual guidance and to seek their advice and help in the problems and difficulties which confronted them. Not only the learned and cultured among them, but at times the grim Stylite also have made their influence felt in the councils of emperors and magistrates.

In times of crisis whole bodies of monks would rise in the

defence of Orthodoxy as they knew it, and even impose their will by force or the threat of it. Such was the unedifying spectacle at the "Robber-Synod" of Ephesus, and the Bishop of Alexandria in the hey-dey of his power could always count upon such support. On the other hand the corporate influence exerted by the monastic order is to be seen in a much more favourable light when the monks took the lead in the defence of the images under Theodore of the monastery of Studius in the iconoclastic controversy. They suffered for their fearless insistence upon their principles, both in respect of the images themselves, and in regard to the intrusion of the Emperor into the sphere of spiritual discipline.

The ideals of the monastic life were lofty, but human nature remains weak and fallible. It is not to be expected that those ideals would always be reached, nor even the struggle to reach them always be maintained. It would seem to be the experience of monastic life in general that it is subject to periods in which the monks tend to get lax in the practice of their ascetic ideals. Such occasions give rise sometimes to reform and the bracing effects of a return to the stringency of earlier standards, and sometimes to a modification of rule in recognition of human frailty. It was in one such period that a new form of the monastic life established itself on Mount Athos in the fifteenth century. It is known as *Idiorrhythmism*, a word which means roughly "living in one's own way". Idiorrhythmic monks claim, and have succeeded in establishing, the right to hold private property. In such monasteries there is no abbot, control is exercised by a Council of monks, the head of which is elected yearly. Each monk receives a certain amount of food and a small sum of money from the monastery, and he earns by his own work whatever he wants or needs in addition. Thus while the rule of celibacy and the rule of obedience are maintained, the rule of poverty is virtually abrogated.

Nearly half the monasteries of Mount Athos are Idiorhythmic and this modified form of the common life has spread elsewhere in the Orthodox world.

In the fourteenth century a peculiar aspect of Orthodox monasticism came to the forefront, became the subject of lively controversy for a decade, and finally received official approval. This was *hesychasm*. The word means quietude and alludes to the state of interior quiet which the contemplative sought to attain. There was a time in the sixth century when hesychast simply meant monk, but later the name was restricted to the contemplative solitary and the hermit, the type of monk which the regulations drawn up by St. Basil, the Emperor Justinian, and others, had tended to discourage, although without forbidding it.

Hesychasm was not new in the fourteenth century. It was a tradition which claimed descent through Simeon the New Theologian, a great visionary and mystic who died in 1022, he belonged to the monastery of Studius, and his writings had much influence upon Orthodox monasticism. Its great champion Gregory who took the habit on Mount Sinai in 1330, and later went to Mount Athos, appealed also to St. John of the Ladder, a sixth-century mystic, and other writers on the ascetic life. Indeed from the earliest days there had been men who aspired to the joys of mystical contemplation and wrote of the methods by which these were to be attained, with theories of the mystical light and a system of partly physical methods of inducing it.

> "When thou art alone in thy cell, shut thy door, and seat thyself in a corner; raise thy mind above all things vain and transitory; recline thy beard and chin on thy breast; turn thine eyes and thy thought towards the middle of thy belly, the region of the navel and search the place of the heart, the seat of the soul. At first all will be dark and comfortless, but if thou persevere day and night, thou wilt feel an ineffable joy; and no sooner has the soul discovered the place of the heart than it is involved in a mystic and ethereal light."

So Gibbon cites[1] an eleventh century Athonite abbot.

Here the desire of Orthodox monastic practice to see and to feel comes to a head. For the reward of such contemplation was held by the hesychasts to be the very substance of God Himself, the uncreated light revealed on Mount Tabor at the Transfiguration.

[1] *Decline and Fall*, Chapter 63.

A highly cultivated monk named Barlaam who had lived
t the Court of Avignon but was now back in Constantinople,
nd who paid a visit to Athos, denounced such a doctrine as
candalous and heretical; for it implied in his view two sub-
tances in the Godhead, one visible and the other invisible.

But the theology, if not the cruder practice of hesychasm,
ound an able defender in St. Gregory Palamas who later be-
ame Archbishop of Thessalonika. Hesychasm spread and
ound a second home in Bulgaria. The controversy raged for
ome years, more than one Council considered the subject, and
he hesychasts won in the end. In the civil war between John
Cantacuzenus and John Palaeologus the support of the popular
nd venerated monks of Athos was of importance. And the
urprising end was that the unchanging East, with all its pride
f intact tradition and its horror of innovation, formally accepted
he new doctrine of the uncreated light of Mount Tabor at a
Council held in Constantinople in 1351. Hesychasm has held
he place it thus secured in Orthodox monasticism. It was at
Mount Athos that the Russian Nil Sorsky learned its doctrine,
nd incorporated the best of it into his own thought, whence
t flowed into the stream of Russian monastic life.

Some centres of Orthodox monasticism claim special
ttention.

The Monastery of St. Katharine on Mount Sinai ranks
s one of the autocephalous Churches of the Orthodox Communion and its Abbot has the title of Archbishop. Near the
ocky summit of this "God-trodden" mountain, sacred to
slam and to the Jews as well as to Christians, whither,
ccording to legend, angels carried the body of St. Katharine
f Alexandria after her martyrdom, Justinian built in 550 the
amous monastery which stands today much as his builders
eft it. The Emperor endowed the foundation generously and
ince his day many benefactors have bestowed liberal gifts
pon it, so that, exempt as it has been from taxation under all
olitical régimes, the monastery grew very wealthy. It
ossesses a library which is rich in manuscripts, and it was
here that in 1844 Tischendorf made his famous discovery
f the Codex Sinaiaticus, the fourth century manuscript of
he New Testament now in the British Museum, which

purchased it from the Russian Government for £100,000. In early days the Monastery of Mount Sinai was under the jurisdiction sometimes of Jerusalem and sometimes of Alexandria. A synod of 1782, however, formally recognized its complete independence, although the Archbishop is always consecrated by the Patriarch of Jerusalem. He lives in Cairo The monastery has a number of daughter-houses here and there in the world of Orthodoxy. One of them flourished for two hundred years in the Island of Crete and produced some famous men, among them Cyril Lucar. The Archbishop of Sinai has no lay flock, and apart from its sacred association and interesting history the fact that the small body of monks under his jurisdiction constitutes an independent Church on the same footing in that respect as, for example, the immense Church of Russia with its many million adherents, gives it a unique interest.

But Orthodoxy has innumerable monasteries and even the briefest account cannot omit mention of the ancient religious houses of Judaea and Cyprus or of the romantic monasteries of which Curzon wrote, some of which, as at Metéora, are perched on the top of cliffs so inaccessible that the visitor is drawn up by a rope.

Russia has its famous monastery of the Holy Trinity near Moscow with its fortified walls which has played an important part in Russian history. It was here that Dmitry of the Don took counsel with St. Sergius before sallying forth to his great fight with the Tartars, and here was the rallying centre of Russian patriotism under Minin the butcher and Pozharsky the Prince, when the Poles had taken Moscow at the beginning of the seventeenth century.

Further south is the ancient fourfold monastery of Kiev with its catacombs, which is probably the place of origin of the basis of the chronicle "of Nestor", now usually known as the Primary Chronicle, the earliest source for the beginnings of Russian history.

There is the great monastery of Pochaev in Volhynia; of Valaam on an island in Lake Ladoga; and away in the far north on another island in the White Sea, is Solovetsky which has the distinction of having been bombarded by an English ship during the Crimean War. The cannon balls are still to be seen there.

These there are, and many more, some of which have, in their day, been outposts of civilization and centres of missionary activity, and within whose walls century after century individual men have led lives of asceticism, hard work and prayer.

But the heart of Orthodox monasticism and indeed the devotional heart of Orthodoxy as a whole is Mount Athos, and this may be described in somewhat greater detail as representing Orthodox monasticism *par excellence*.

On the northern shores of the Aegean Sea the Thracian Chersonesus stretches out three fingers which point southwards. The eastern of these three is the one which Xerxes cut through in 483 B.C. in order to bring his fleet to Athens without having to risk the stormy passage round it. At its tip this rocky finger of land rises to a peak of 6,000 feet. This is Mount Athos, the Holy Mountain of Orthodoxy. Athos has its place both in classical mythology and in Christian legend, but its history as a centre of Christian monasticism does not begin before the ninth century. There were then, and perhaps earlier, hermits living there: they may have come as refugees during the iconoclast controversy. The monks of Athos were recognized by an imperial charter of 875. But the organization of monastic life on the mountain was due to a certain St. Athanasius who died in A.D. 1000, after establishing, with the help of the Emperor Nicephorus Phocas, the first, and still the chief, of the Athonite monasteries, the Lavra.

Mount Athos enjoyed the favour of succeeding Emperors of Byzantium and prospered exceedingly in spite of attacks by pirates and Latins and other foes from outside. More and more monasteries were built. As early as 1094 Athos was declared independent of the neighbouring bishoprics of Ierosos and Salonika, and it became a sort of monastic republic. Of the twenty sovereign monasteries which have survived to the present day nineteen had been established by the middle of the fourteenth century. The twentieth (*Stavronikéta*) was founded two hundred years later, and is the only one of them, therefore, which is not an imperial foundation. At the present time they are all under the direct jurisdiction of the Ecumenical Patriarch and so belong to the class of monastery known as

K

Stavropegion, from the ceremonial of placing upon the altar a cross (stavros) sent by the Patriarch when such churches are consecrated. Apart from one Serb, one Bulgarian and the huge Russian establishment of St. Panteleimon, all the monasteries are Greek. Eleven of them are coenobitic and the other nine idiorrhythmic. Among them the twenty monasteries own all the land of the Athonite peninsula, upon which, as is well known, no female creature is allowed to set foot.[1] Some concession seems to be made in favour of hens.

By no means all the monks of the mountain live, however, within the sovereign monasteries. There are a number of other forms of the monastic life to be found there. There are twelve recognized *Sketai*, one of them is Georgian and another Rumanian. A *skêtê* is a group of small houses with a church and dependant upon a monastery. In theory it is a much smaller unit though in one or two cases it has outgrown the parent house. A cell is a still smaller unit than a *skêtê*, and is inhabited by two or three monks who support themselves from the soil and pay rent to the monastery for it; while the hermit lives in a tiny "kathisma" and the extreme ascetic in some inaccessible retreat known as a "hesychasterion".

Under the constitution which dates from 1783 and was revised in 1924, the affairs of the whole community of Mount Athos are managed by a legislative body which consists of one representative elected yearly from each of the twenty sovereign monasteries. They meet in the village of Karyes which has been the seat of government since the tenth century. There is also an executive committee of four, chosen annually, one from each of a group of four monasteries taken in turn. Since there are five such groups, each monastery is represented on the executive every five years. The members of the executive are not members of the legislative body, but the president of the one is also the chairman of the other.

On the whole the monks have fared well enough in their relations with secular rulers, at least until modern times. When the Turks captured Salonika in 1430 and secured control of

---

[1] For the probable reason of this regulation, which was first promulgated by St. Plato (uncle of St. Theodore of the Studium, who adopted it) in his monastery at Saccoudion, see Baynes and Moss, *Byzantium*, p. 149.

Athos they respected the privileges of the monks in return for a substantial tribute. Athos suffered severely when the Turks occupied it during the Greek War of Independence; and still more in 1861 when Prince Cuza confiscated the vast estates in Rumania which pious benefactors in the past had bestowed upon the monasteries. Some indemnity was offered but the monks regarded the whole transaction as purely illegal, and refused it. The loss to them was an income of £120,000 a year, which meant the severe impoverishment of fourteen of the richest monasteries. These were Greek, and one effect was to tilt the balance in favour of the Russians in the perennial rivalry and friction which has existed between Russians and Greeks in the history of the Holy Mountain. But the turn of the Russians was to come, and the Russian Revolution has left the Russian monks on Athos almost entirely destitute.

The Greek census of 1928 gave the total number of monks on Athos as 4,858, rather less than half of whom reside within the walls of the monasteries. The monasteries are all fortified, and grouped among the luxuriant foliage they provide a picture of great beauty. The typical monastery surrounds a courtyard in the centre of which is the church and at one end the refectory. A fountain stands between them. The surrounding walls enclose on the ground floor store rooms and offices, and the monks' living quarters in the two or three stories above. The walls are castellated and may have projecting wooden galleries. In one corner is the keep, now generally converted into a library. The monastic libraries are rich in manuscripts and other documents which, even after the losses incurred during the Greek War of Independence, and by fire and neglect, are of great value to the political, ecclesiastical and social historian, and Athos is a store house of treasures of Byzantine art.

The monks spend their time for the most part in religious exercises. Otherwise they occupy themselves with agriculture, fishing and handicrafts.

The ideal of the Orthodox monk is to glorify God and to save his own soul by a life of prayer and mortification. They all follow with greater or less strictness the system of St. Basil. There is nothing to correspond with the variety of Orders and

Congregations which have developed in the West. The Orthodox monks do not fail in the duty of showing charity to the poor, and hospitality to the traveller. Benevolent institutions, such as schools and hospitals, may be attached to a monastery, in the sense that they are supported by funds provided by it, but not in the sense that the monks themselves give personal service in them. The fulfilment of an apostolate to the world is no part of the primary purpose of the Orthodox in embracing the monastic life. An exception is provided by many of the monks of mediaeval Russia. Here too it may be true that their first object in pushing their settlements ever further into the remote and barbarous districts to the north and east, was to escape from the world and secure that solitude in which the contemplative life can thrive. But it is to their honour that when so placed they were not deaf to the call of the world around them. These Russian monastic settlements were lights shining in the darkness and became civilizing and evangelizing agencies of incalculable worth among the peoples of the steppes and the tundras.

Nor must the intellectual and artistic activities of the religious houses of Orthodoxy be overlooked. The work of their copyists has saved the contents of many an ancient manuscript from being lost to posterity. Religious literature has been enriched by the original writings of Orthodox monks on theology, mysticism, prayer and the ascetic life, and they compiled many lives of the saints.

The religious poetry which figures so prominently in Orthodox forms of worship is largely the work of monks. Much of it is of great beauty and some few instances have been translated and established themselves in the hymn books of the West.[1]

Side by side with this is the work of the painter monks who created a whole world of beauty and spirituality of their own in the production of icons and the frescoing of the walls of churches, while the delicate labours of the miniaturist and illuminator of manuscripts have made something precious for the rest of the world.

[1] See Chapter VIII.

CHAPTER XI

ORTHODOXY AND THE PEOPLE

There is evidence that in Russia the year 1948 was marked by widespread religious revival. It is striking and even startling. It tells of the people flocking back to their Church; of very great numbers crowding the churches of Moscow to make their communions during Lent; of physically exhausted priests snatching a few hours' sleep without leaving church, so many were the people who came to seek their ministrations.

Even if such reports exaggerated the facts and were only partly true, they draw attention once more to the ineradicably religious nature of the Russians. They suggest that it is to the temper of the Russian folk as a whole that the West must look for the prospect of peace and mutual understanding, and inspire the hope that in the long run the character of the Russian people will make itself felt and say its say.

In dealing with Orthodoxy we are dealing with a different civilization from our own. It is, if we adopt Toynbee's classification, Byzantine whilst ours is Western, and although both are derived from the Greco-Roman civilization which preceded them, the two have their own characteristic and sometimes divergent views of life. It behoves us then to try to understand the Orthodox view of life, and what especially concerns us here is the mainspring of that view of life—for its mainspring is religion, even if that should manifest itself in negative form, as recently in Russia.

Leaving on one side then the official body of doctrine and the questions which confront the hierarchy in their relations with the State and with those who lie outside the confines of Orthodoxy, what does religion mean when it means anything, to the people of the Orthodox Church, to the man behind the machine, to the worker in the fields, to the housewife and the mother who teaches her children the Orthodox faith?

All generalizations are perilous and break down somewhere. There are marked differences between Greek and Slav, and again within the Slavs themselves. For instance, the Southern Slavs have perhaps never been the enthusiastic churchgoers that their cousins the Russians have been.

If we ask in what manner a man is conscious of his religion we shall get different answers. In some religions he is conscious of it in terms of fear. The Western man or woman is probably aware of it primarily in terms of duty, of the claims it makes upon him in respect of conduct. I am talking about its primary impact and his immediate response, if he makes any. Doubtless many other things follow.

But one might perhaps risk the assertion that the Orthodox are conscious of their religion primarily in terms of the reality of the unseen world and the permeation of this world by the other. Orthodoxy is meeting, the meeting of two worlds, the contact of the material and the spiritual and even the penetration of the material by the spiritual.

When the Greek stands in Church, this is what he is aware of and here he finds it symbolized. The space where he stands, before the Iconostas, is this world, behind the Iconostas, is the other world. There they meet and there, as he makes his communion, they meet again not in symbol but in fact, in his own person. The icon which he salutes in reverence, he looks not at, but through, for it is (among other things) a window opening upon the spiritual world.

All this is because God Himself came from the heavenly world and entered the earthly, and what is more, stayed in it. The faith, the doctrinal statements to which all alike, both clergy and laity, adhere so passionately, are but the safeguarding shrine of this commanding truth and all that it implies.

This explains the central position which Easter occupies in the spiritual life of Orthodoxy. The Great Service takes place at midnight and it has been frequently described. It is preceded by a procession outside the Church, which represents a fruitless search for the body of Christ. Then follow the joyful announcement "Christ is Risen", and the Easter Liturgy to which succeed domestic rejoicings which may last most of the night. For Christ has plunged into the abysses of this world and deeper still, to return with the new life of restorative power which shall claim not only the hearts of men but the whole cosmos for light and truth. Fedotov[1] draws attention to the figure of Cosmos in Greek icons which represent the out-pouring of the Holy Spirit at Pentecost. The Apostles are grouped around Our Lady in the upper room and the flickering tongues of fire play upon the head of each, and there is another figure in the picture who also shares in the out-pouring of the Spirit. It is "King Cosmos", a crowned and bearded man who is apparently coming up from below, out of the earth.

But it is expressed and preserved in other more homely and intimate ways, and the Church's touch upon Nature is repeated as the year unfolds. New mown hay, just as it is with the flowers that fell with it, is brought in armfuls and strewn on the floor of the church at Whitsuntide, for Pentecost was one of the first of Harvest Festivals. On the Feast of the Transfiguration which means much for Orthodoxy, grapes are blessed and distributed. "As the water is changed by Nature into the blood of the grape," a Serb said to me, "so by a higher power the blood of the grape is changed into the Blood of Christ." Once more that world penetrates this to transfigure and enrich it.

A ceremony to which enthusiastic crowds always flock, and which may be seen in any Orthodox land from the Jordan to the Neva, is the Blessing of the Waters at the Epiphany. It commemorates the Baptism of Christ, but as it has spread from Palestine into the rest of the Orthodox world, so it has widened its significance to include the touch of the other world upon the waters which give life and fruitfulness to the earth. And a charming ceremony it is, best seen perhaps in the cold countries where at that season of the year the rivers are frozen. There great blocks of ice are cut out of the surface, and from them an altar is built, the cross upon which is also fashioned from ice. The vested clergy and their attendants are grouped around and with them the crowds of worshippers and sightseers.

[1] Fedotov: *The Russian Religious Mind*, Harvard, 1946, p. 369.

The waters are blessed by dipping the cross into them with the appropriate prayers. At the Jordan, multitudes of the excited people plunge into the newly blessed river, and even in cold climates there are hardy enthusiasts who will leap through the hole in the ice.[1]

All this and much more is the happy side of the realization that the unseen world of light and life enters into this other dark gross world of sin and suffering. But there is another aspect of it which finds expression in what is a characteristic cry of Orthodoxy—"*Lord have mercy.*"

Toynbee has written[2] that one element in Russia's inheritance from Byzantium is the conviction that Byzantium, and then Russia is always right. In matters of State policy, both secular and ecclesiastical, this may well be so. But there is a sense in which the Orthodox has the conviction that he is always wrong. Not only is he aware of his failures and shortcomings in his relations with his fellows, but he expresses it. A Russian in saying "good-bye" to a friend may use a word which equally well means "forgive". If he is a devout person, he may seek his acquaintances and ask their forgiveness, not necessarily with any specific wrongdoing in his mind, on solemn occasions, as, for instance, when he intends to make his communion. A vivid sense of man's need of the divine compassion of forgiveness is woven into the very fabric of Orthodox religion. The words "Lord have mercy" are constantly on the lips of the Orthodox and they are repeated, over and over again in the course of worship.

The scene may be in a cathedral church on September 14, the Festival of the Exaltation of the Cross. A platform has been erected in the centre of the church, and upon this a group of men stand. They hold in their hands a huge and resplendent cross. Very slowly, by almost imperceptible degrees they raise it, holding it in a vertical position, and lifting it higher and higher, until they can reach no further. The cross remains for a moment, poised at its highest elevation, above the heads of the bearers, above the watching eyes of the

[1] In Greece a cross is thrown into the sea with a ribbon attached by which it is retrieved. In town churches the ceremony of blessing the water may take place at the font.

[2] *Civilization on Trial*, p. 164 ff., Oxford, 1948.

vast multitude of worshippers who throng the church on all sides. Then with the same slow deliberation it is gradually lowered again to the ground. During this action a choir is singing, and many of the congregation whispering—"Lord have mercy"—just that one phrase over and over again, beginning softly on a very low note and rising in pitch and increasing in volume until the cross is at its maximum height, when the whole building reverberates with the reiterated appeal which slowly dies away again as the cross descends. Then the whole action is repeated to the same accompaniment, and more than once. The number of repetitions must run into hundreds. To many Western minds they will doubtless appear "vain repetitions". But the look on the faces of the worshippers will perhaps give pause to the expression of any such sentiment. The dramatic action expresses something very deeply implanted in the religious consciousness of the Orthodox, the feeling of human unworthiness and its need of the divine compassion, the sense of being imprisoned in the dark and crude elements of this world and the appeal for light and liberation.

Closely allied to it is the awareness of a positive value in suffering and humility, even of humiliation. One meets many members of the Orthodox Church whom political events and recent decades have reduced from riches to poverty or from a reasonable degree of material comfort to almost none at all. But very rarely indeed is there any sign of bitterness and resentment in their reaction. The vivid awareness of the other world does much to soften the asperities of this, and that unseen world is peopled by those who have suffered, it is ruled by the Christ Who humbled Himself.

Another scene may illustrate this, the ceremony of the feet-washing on Maundy Thursday—which again will pack the church to the doors and beyond. A large dais has been erected in the centre and on it are twelve seats in two rows facing each other. Upon each seat is a bishop fully vested. At a certain point in the service, the chief bishop present, who has been conducting it, lays aside his episcopal vestments, girds himself with a towel and takes a basin and water. He ascends the dais and goes to each of the seated bishops in turn,

kneels in front of him, removes his foot-gear first from on
foot, then from the other, and washes and dries his feet. H
replaces the socks and shoes and passes on to the next. Whe
he comes to the one who represents St. Peter, the latter make
the protest recorded in St. John's Gospel and his reluctanc
has to be overborne before his feet are washed. Finally th
officiant resumes his vestments and the main service continue
its course. How long does all this take? It does not matter, n
one minds or even notices how long. It is all done in absolut
silence. All that is audible is the breathing of one's immediat
neighbours among the tense crowd of worshippers.

Here too is something particularly real to the Orthodo
spirit which is an echo of individual experience, or at least o
individual aspiration constantly known. Humiliation ma
even be sought after from religious motives, and exceptionall
this may take oddly extreme forms. The bizarre and well
nigh incredible figure whom the Russians call "Yurodivi"
which may be translated the "Fool for Christ's sake"[1] coul
only be found within the Eastern Orthodox world. He may b
really deficient mentally, and as such, in the Russian view
under the special protection of God. He may also be the ma
who in pursuit of humility and in praise of it deliberatel
assumed a character of foolishness, and courted the jeers o
those he met, inviting their mockery as he roamed fron
village to village—a fantastic figure, but one who has his mee
of reverence too, for the grace that he seeks is loved.

The Orthodox has more to remind him of the unseen worl
than those who dwell in lands in which religion assumes form
that are more austere. Though for centuries under Turkis
rule he was deprived of such outward signs of religion, so tha
at times he was wont to build his church half buried in th
ground to aid concealment, yet with the return of freedom h
set up his shrines at street corners and along the wayside
Icons are not confined to the churches, they are to be foun
in the houses, in every room of a devout household. Th
living-room will have an icon in a position stereotyped b
custom, and a visitor will salute it on entering as he greets hi
host. Especially in Russia of pre-revolution days, icons wer

[1] See 1 Corinthians iv, 10.

be seen everywhere, at the railway stations, in the shops, prisons and barracks and all sorts of public buildings.

A further reminder is provided by events in the yearly round marked by the Church Kalendar. This has perhaps a more intimate touch upon the lives of Orthodox people, so many of whom are peasants for whom the festivals of the Church are closely associated with the recurrent seasons in Nature and with agricultural work.

The Orthodox Kalendar is in its framework the same as the Western. That is to say it is built up around the Great Festivals which are common to the whole of Christendom, Easter being the chief of all. But there is no Trinity Sunday, the first Sunday after Whitsuntide is used by the Orthodox for the commemoration of All Saints. Thereafter the Sundays are counted after Whit Sunday. In the course of the year many of the Sundays are given names, e.g., the first Sunday after Easter is known as the Sunday of St. Thomas, and in general the names are derived from the Gospel appointed for the day. The first Sunday in Lent is Orthodox Sunday (see p. 54) when blessings are invoked upon the champions of Orthodoxy and anathemas upon its foes. There is no season of Advent.

Every day is marked as the commemoration of a saint, and sometimes of more than one. Here differences will be found in various parts of the Orthodox world owing to the introduction of the names of local saints, and the differences from the West are remarkable. The Orthodox Kalendar contains the names of most of the Old Testament Prophets and Patriarchs and almost none of the Western saints find a place in it. If it is compared with the English Kalendar it will be found that practically none of the minor saints belong to both Kalendars. An outstanding exception is St. George on April 23, who is highly venerated in the East as the Great Martyr.

The times of fasting prescribed by the Orthodox Church are more frequent than in any part of the West. In addition to Lent, which begins in the East on the Monday after Quinquagesima, and is known as the Great Lent, another fasting period is the first fortnight of August, another is the six weeks before Christmas, and there is still another of varying length

between the octave of Whit Sunday and June 29, the festiva
of St. Peter and Paul.

Even outside these periods there are many days upor
which the Orthodox faithful are expected to use only abstinence
food, including, with a few exceptions, all Wednesdays and
Fridays.

Furthermore, fasting itself is a much more rigorous affai
among the Orthodox than it is in the West. It involves
abstinence from any food of animal origin including fish,
milk, eggs and butter. Indeed, the strict observer is left with
little but bread, fruit and vegetables.

The extent to which this formidable programme is actually
carried out is difficult to estimate. Doubtless like other
observances of religion it has less hold upon people than it
had, and town dwellers sit more lightly to it than the peasantry
Nevertheless, the Orthodox probably fulfil their obligation in
this respect to an extent which would surprise the easy-going
Westerner. Many of the devout are strict about it, and those
who practise their religion at all will observe at least the first
and last few days of the prescribed periods of fasting.

To the Orthodox, religion is very much concerned with this
world as well as with the next, and fasting is of importance
not only as a discipline of the human will. It expresses also the
impact of the spiritual upon the material, the control of the
world which is seen, by the power of the unseen world. It
plays its part in causing the material to serve spiritual ends
and thus the human will shares in the process of rescuing and
restoring the fallen world of Nature.

The clergy are a visible link between the two worlds. The
parish priest with his flowing cassock and unshorn hair stand
apart. He is and is seen to be distinct from other men. He is
reminder of the unseen spiritual world in which both he and
his flock are living even while they live in the day-to-day world
of material things, and his ministrations apply the power of
the spirit to daily life.

Yet if he stands apart, he does not stand aloof. The
parochial clergy throughout the Orthodox East are required
to be married men. But they must marry before they are
ordained. Once they are ordained marriage is forbidden them

Very frequently they marry the daughters of other priests, and thus clerical families tend to form a fairly well defined section of the community with its own traditions and general outlook. But in the country districts at any rate, and that is to say in the vast majority of cases, they live a life which is close to that of their parishioners. It is a simple life; they cultivate their own piece of land, and are not regarded as belonging to gentry. The question naturally arises, what happens if a parish priest is left a widower? Being a parish priest, he must have a wife, being ordained, he is precluded from marrying. In strict theory there is nothing for it but for him to give up his parish and retire into a monastery. But the theory is not unduly pressed, and he may even be allowed to have a female relation to look after his children. The bishops, on the other hand, are always chosen from among the monks, and they, of course, must remain unmarried. The married cleric can reach no higher dignity than that of Arch-priest. So that at the outset of his career the neophyte must make up his mind whether he will take a wife and settle down to parish work—or whether he will take the monastic vows and keep open the possibility of being made a bishop later on. Transition from one class to another is not common, but there are cases of widowed priests entering a monastery and subsequently being raised to episcopal rank.

The deacon is as familiar to the people as the priest, for the diaconate is not regarded in the East as a mere step towards the priesthood and expected to last only about a year. So far from being simply a sort of incomplete priest, the Greek or Russian deacon may remain in deacon's orders all his life, and he very frequently does. He has a well-defined status with its own specific function. The deacon has his own assigned part in the Liturgy, notably the chanting of the Litanies and the singing of the Gospel; one of his qualifications is the possession of a good voice. "Father Deacon" shares in the respect and affection which are commonly given to the parish priest. Should it unhappily be the case that the priest or deacon is not all that he ought to be and even notoriously otherwise, the people will not on that account stop going to Church. If you have a good priest, so much the better, thank God that it is as it should be. If you have a bad one, that is much to be deplored. But a priest of some sort you must have, for otherwise there are no worship and no sacraments, and these are just where, most conspicuously, the other world breaks through.

As the Church, with its succession of festivals and fast keeps touch with the yearly cycle of Nature, so it shepherd the individual human life from the cradle to the grave. The rites that attend his birth and his death stress the link between the two worlds, and the fact that man lives in both at the same time. Even his baptism is not the first occasion on which a child of Orthodox parents will be brought into contact with the Church of which he is to become a member. On the day following the birth the priest comes to say prayers over the mother and child, and again a week later when the child is given his name. On the fortieth day from its birth the mother brings the child to Church, when prayers are said for the child, and if baptism has meanwhile been administered the priest carries the child through the church and (in the case of a male child) into the Sanctuary, reciting the *Nunc Dimittis*. But unless the child has been baptized at home, which is not infrequently the case, the latter ceremony will follow baptism. And the prayers of the eighth day are now combined with those of the first day. The rite of baptism is preceded by exorcism and a short catechism of renunciation of Satan and acceptance of Christ, which concludes with the recitation of the Nicene Creed.

The administration of the Sacrament itself begins with a Litany said by the deacon while the priest prays secretly for himself and for the one about to be baptized. This is followed by a long prayer said aloud, in the course of which the water is blessed in words which at times recall the phraseology of the Anglican rite; e.g.,

> "Grant that the person to be baptized therein may be thoroughly renewed, that he may put off the old man which is corrupt through deceitful lusts and put on the new man after the image of him that made him; that being planted in the likeness of his death by baptism, he may be partaker of his resurrection."

Olive oil is then blessed, the surface of the water signed with it, and the child is anointed. With his fingers dipped in the oil, the priest signs the child on the brow, saying

"The servant of God, *N.*, is anointed with the oil of gladness in the Name of the Father and of the Son and of the Holy Ghost. Amen. Unto the healing of soul and body" (here the sign is made on the breast and back). "Unto hearing the faith" (on the ears). "Thy hands have made me and fashioned me" (on the palms). "That he may walk in the way of Thy commandments" (on the feet).

The child is then baptized with threefold immersion and the words, "The Servant of God, *N.*, is baptized in the Name of the Father, Amen. And of the Son, Amen. And of the Holy Ghost, Amen."

The Baptism ended, Chrism, which corresponds with the Western Confirmation, follows immediately. It begins with an ascription of praise and thanksgiving for the baptismal gift, merging into a prayer for "the seal of the gift of thy holy, and almighty, and adorable Spirit." The child is then anointed[1] in the sign of the cross on the brow, eyes, nostrils, lips, ears, breast, hands and feet; and at each anointing the priest says, "The seal of the Gift of the Holy Spirit. Amen."

A triple circuit of the font is then made with lighted tapers by the clergy and the sponsors carrying the child, the circle thus made symbolizes unbroken and eternal union with Christ. Thereafter the child is entitled, even as an infant, to receive Communion. Startling as this may be to Western minds, he may, in fact, be brought to church for this purpose once or twice a year from his baptism onwards. It emphasizes what is sometimes called the "given-ness" of the Christian religion. As the infant is capable of receiving the Grace of God in baptism, though he is totally unaware of what is happening,

---

[1] Not with simple olive oil again, but with chrism, which contains a large number of ingredients and is prepared with elaborate ceremonial by the chief bishop during Holy Week once every few years as required. The consecration of this chrism was from the thirteenth or fourteenth century onwards claimed by the Ecumenical Patriarch as his sole right. In modern times the claim has been contested and some of the Orthodox Churches consecrate the chrism for their own use.

so he may be considered able to receive the divine gifts i
Communion. His dawning consciousness is trained to accep
the privilege of meeting the other world as it there break
through into this. When he is seven years old he is expecte
to make his first Confession, as he learns another side to th
matter—his own unworthiness and responsibilities.

Nor does the care of the Church for the individual ceas
with his physical death, though it is much concentrated upo
that moment. In cases of grave sickness (though not onl
in articulo mortis) or in view of some special risk of death, th
devout Orthodox may be the recipient of the Sacrament o
Holy Unction, and be anointed, with prayers for his recover
or safety. The long service is abbreviated in practice.

When a death occurs the house will be visited, even o
three successive days by the priest and the prescribed servic
said in the presence of the body. The actual funeral service i
Church is penetrated by the sense of the pathos of this lif
and of hope in the life to come. It contains passages of incom
parable beauty, such as the first of the *ideomela* of St. Joh
Damascene:

> "What delight of life continueth unmixed with sorrow
> What glory on earth remaineth unalterable? All things ar
> more fleeting than a shadow, all things are more illusiv
> than dreams; one moment, and all these things are suc
> ceeded by Death. But in the light of Thy countenanc
> and in the sweetness of Thy beauty, do Thou, O Chris
> in mercy, give rest to *him* whom Thou hast chosen, foras
> much as Thou art the lover of mankind.[1]

And the Church's pastoral care for the devout believe
reaches out to him beyond the grave. There are ceremoni
prescribed for the eighth and the fortieth day after death a
well as for the anniversary. For according to popular beli
the soul does not bid a final farewell to this world until for
days after death, the interval having been spent in visiting th
scenes of its earthly life, and even Mt. Athos and Jerusalen

[1] See a translation of the Burial Service published by Douglas Pepl
Ditchling, 1922, and with the above quotation *cf.* No. 360 in *The Engl
Hymnal*.

Food and drink for the departed play their part in the rites for the dead, especially the grains of wheat which are now taken to symbolize the resurrection. But in the religious life of the people, Christianity has often had to come to terms with tough survivals among old pagan customs which it more or less disguises, particularly in the picturesque domestic ceremonies which often follow the more orthodox proceedings in Church. This is true not only of the rites which accompany death, but of many other observances also in the course of the year. They may not stand the test of rigid Orthodox belief, and the parish priest, who is perhaps better educated than the members of his flock, may frown upon them, but at least they have a humble part to play in reminding the peasant of the reality of the unseen world and that he is but a pilgrim in this.

Pilgrimage too in the literal sense figures prominently in the religion of the people. The desire to go on pilgrimage is felt by every faithful Orthodox believer. It may be only to the neighbouring monastery or the shrine of a local saint. It may be much further afield, and happy is he who realizes the ideal of every devout pilgrim, and journeys to the Holy Land. But whether the goal be near or far, the pilgrim goes to confess his sins, to say his prayers and to eat, drink and be merry at some place where the unseen world has markedly broken through and made it holy.

L

CHAPTER XII

ORTHODOXY IN THE MODERN WORLD

THE modern expansion of Orthodoxy begins with the romantic story of the Russian conquest of Siberia which was begun by Yermak in the reign of Ivan the Terrible (1582). The Russian, as Berdyaev often notes, is essentially a pilgrim and a wanderer, and when he wanders abroad he takes his Church with him. Thus, Orthodoxy has spread north-eastward, right across Siberia and even into Japan, where one of the most striking foreign missions in the history of Christendom led to the establishment of a Japanese Orthodox Church. Its Metropolitan claimed 40,000 adherents in 1931, and all its clergy were Japanese. The Orthodox communities on the mainland of northeast Asia have grown greatly both in size and in importance since the Russian Revolution in 1917 drove many refugees and settlers into that part of the world. The vast diocese of Harbin includes adherents of various races, but they are mainly Russians. Nor did the movement stop at the confines of Asia.

By way of the Aleutian Islands and Alaska, Orthodoxy was introduced into the American Continent at the end of the eighteenth century. The Russians were thus the first to bring Orthodoxy to the New World, but since then members of other Orthodox nations—Greeks, Albanians, Rumanians, Serbs and others—have joined in the flood of immigration from the Old World, and the Orthodox Church has travelled to America, journeying from east to west as well as from west to east. A Russian diocese was founded in South America in 1934. Before the second world war there were eleven Russian dioceses on the American Continent and four Greek. The Orthodox bishops in the United States in a letter to President Roosevelt claimed to speak as representing six million people.[1] It is a significant fact that Athenagoras, the Greek Archbishop of America was in 1948 elected to the Ecumenical Throne of Constantinople. There is a Greek Orthodox diocese also in Australia, its archbishop resides in Sydney. Orthodox who live in South Africa too belong to a Greek diocese with its archbishop at Johannesburg. It is one of the seven dioceses of the Patriarchate of Alexandria, whereas the Australian diocese belongs to Constantinople.

Nor must the Russian *diaspora* which followed the Revolution be forgotten. It led to the formation or the enlargement of colonies of Russian Orthodox in many cities of Central and Western Europe with the establishment of diocesan life outside Russia whose relation to the Mother Church in Moscow still remains unsettled.

Thus Orthodoxy is a world-wide phenomenon. Its significance cannot be fairly assessed only in terms of its homelands in the east of Europe. There, of course, the enormous majority of its adherents live, and there is the traditional centre of its prestige. But in considering on the one hand the impact of the modern world upon Orthodoxy and on the other hand any message that Orthodoxy may have for the post-war world, those scattered communities of Orthodox over the world cannot be left out of account.

The parallel with the Anglican Communion can hardly escape notice. That too, like the Orthodox, is made up of a number of independent self-governing Churches, each managing its own affairs, but all in communion with each other and finding their centre of unity in Canterbury as the Orthodox find theirs in Constantinople.

Thus Orthodoxy has come increasingly into contact with "the West", and members of other Christian Confessions have opportunities of becoming aware of it and of studying it by personal observation. Such opportunities are, indeed, much limited, but nevertheless Orthodoxy is no longer a remote phenomenon known to the West only through the medium of travellers' reports or the learned writings of experts.

[1] Bolshakoff : *Foreign Missions,* who gives many statistics about Russian Orthodox abroad.

Orthodoxy is in touch with the Ecumenical Movement, and its representatives have taken part in the conferences and assemblies which that movement convenes. Modern Russia, and especially modern Greece, have produced a number of able and erudite theological scholars fully competent to place Orthodoxy in the setting of the modern world. It is characteristic of Orthodoxy that many of its greatest theologians are laymen. For in the Orthodox Church, theological learning is not regarded as a clerical preserve. It is part of that task of guarding and preserving the Faith which is conceived as the function of the whole Church, of the *laos*, the people of God.

But Orthodoxy has been cautious, and to some extent suspicious in its contact with other Confessions. Its readiness to come into closer touch with them has ebbed and flowed. For instance, in 1925 almost the whole Orthodox world was represented at the Nicene Commemoration in London. But in 1948 the Orthodox assembled at Moscow to celebrate the five-hundredth anniversary of the establishment of the independence of the Russian Church, all, with the exception of the representatives of Constantinople and Greece, subscribed to pronouncements which, as well as expressing the traditional Orthodox hostility to the Vatican, were unfavourable both to the recognition of Anglican Orders and to the Ecumenical Movement. They declined to take any part in the meeting of the World Conference of Churches at Amsterdam in that year.

Whether this attitude was to any extent due to political causes and adopted under Russian pressure as consonant with the general cleavage at the time between Russia and the West, is a question which different people will answer with different guesses. But what is beyond question is Orthodox uneasiness at the possibility that the Ecumenical Movement might move towards an attempt to set up a sort of inter-confessional superchurch, which seeks unity through a process of dilution, and accepts as its faith the lowest common denominator of the respective beliefs of those who compose it. In actual fact, Amsterdam itself made it clear that nothing of the kind was contemplated. But the uneasiness exists in the Orthodox mind; and it not only fears that unity may be sought in what they regard as the wrong way, but frankly suspects the motives which inspire the Ecumenical Movement.

In any case, it is well enough known that when the West enters into relation with Orthodoxy it must expect to meet with a conservative attitude. The Orthodox are of course conservative. But theirs is not a conservatism which is rigid and passive, with eyes only for the past and with ears which are deaf to the voices of the modern world. It is not a mummy swathed in the bands of tradition. Theirs is a conservatism which can shew itself surprisingly flexible at times, and it is an active sense of guardianship. Its stress is upon truth rather than upon authority.

For the Orthodox Church conceives itself as the whole Church, and to it is committed the deposit of faith, the truth of the divine revelation, which is one and the same in the first century or the tenth or the twentieth, which is susceptible of explanation, but not of change. The conservatism of Orthodoxy is due to the fear lest this trust should not be fulfilled, lest any generation of Orthodox should hand on to the next less than, or something other than it received. This inherent quality has been emphasized and strengthened by the history of the Orthodox peoples. For all of them have at one time or other, and some for long periods, been subject politically to an alien, hostile and non-Christian despotism when their religious life was their only corporate life, and their Christian faith the symbol of all their hope.

This conception of its life as custodianship, this stress upon truth rather than upon authority is perhaps what saves the relations of Orthodoxy with other Confessions from being a mere demand for submission. There is a wide difference between one bishop's saying "all Christians must submit to my jurisdiction", and the Orthodox "if you hold the same faith as we, you are indeed one with us". "The Faith" is primary, everything else is secondary, and it is of the first importance to grasp this Orthodox point of view. "The first mark of the Church is that all her teachers and pastors agree with each other in everything." This startling assertion was made by Metrophanes Kritopoulos in his *Confession*, which is one of the Symbolic Books of Orthodoxy.

The Faith of the Church is now what it always has been. Dogma is not a fossilized deposit from the minds of the past. It is a living experience of the whole body of the faithful. If you hold the Church's faith and live the Church's life, then you belong to the Church. That is where the stress lies in Orthodoxy. It follows that the great offence against the life of the Church is innovation on the part of any of its members—or group of its members. The idea that since A is true and B is true, and since by the process of logical deduction in human reasoning C follows, therefore C can be erected into a new dogma, is an idea they will not accept. This is the root of their doctrinal quarrel with the Vatican and the distinguishing tenets of Roman Catholicism.

The motive of the Orthodox in entering into discussions with other Christian bodies is perfectly clear. It is two-fold. First to explain their own position, and secondly to ascertain whether those with whom they are conferring do actually hold "the Faith". It is never with the idea of arriving at an amalgam or a mutual adjustment, a working compromise, or an agreed minimum or anything of that kind.

Meanwhile it will be found that they can treat those outside the visible boundaries of Orthodoxy with a surprising degree of accommodation. For in a sense there is no sharply defined edge to Orthodoxy. It is not primarily an institution but a life. It admits of degrees. It may exist to a greater or less extent, or in embryonic form, beyond the limits of the external Orthodox world. The Orthodox hold that the Church (i.e., they themselves) has the power to give an "economic" recognition, under certain conditions, to the sacramental acts of another body of Christians. It is on the strength of this that ministration by Anglican priests to the Orthodox laity and *vice versa* have occurred in different parts of the world. A striking catalogue of such cases could be compiled. On the same ground the Church of Constantinople and some others of the autocephalous Orthodox Churches have recognized Anglican Orders as possessing "the same validity as those of the Roman, Old Catholic, and Armenian Churches possess"; that is to say, not absolutely and in principle, but so far as the Orthodox can judge pending the assurance of identity of faith.

The collapse of humanism and the breakdown of liberalism under the impact of the great wars which have characterized the twentieth century have left a frightening blank in men's minds, and in this state of affairs Orthodoxy has its word to say.

The Greek's own name for their Church is "Orthodox"—they claim to hold unaltered and unimpaired the true doctrine taught and handed on by the Apostles. No less significant is the name by which the Slav members of the same Communion designate it. They call it "Pravoslavny"—the "right-praising" or "right-worshipping" Church. To the Orthodox religion is primarily—though not, of course, solely—belief expressed in worship. Their worship is dogmatic, the truths of their Faith are repeated in it again and again, it re-echoes with glad assertion of what God has done and revealed of Himself in the Christian Gospel, in the experience of the Church, in the lives of the saints.

At the same time it is all couched in the language of poetry and the Service is always sung. The "aesthetic approach" to religion is often spoken of as characteristic of Orthodoxy. There is a legend which was held to explain how Russia came to adopt the religion of Constantinople. Envoys were sent in various directions to investigate different forms of Christianity. Those who had been sent to Constantinople came back and reported on the worship they had witnessed in Justinian's superb Church of the Holy Wisdom. Never had they seen anything like the beauty of it. "We felt we were in heaven rather than on earth," they said. Their description of all this beauty carried the day. "That is the religion for us," cried the Russians.

The truth of this story is in its symbolism. There is in Orthodoxy a real recognition that beauty is one of the links which bind the earth to its Creator. There is much beauty in Orthodox worship, in its buildings, its vestments, its appointments, its music and the quiet unhurried dignity of its movement. Time is of no account in its symbolic representation of the drama of the Life and Death of Christ, and of little account in the actual passing of the moments as anthem and repeated litany unroll themselves. All this is not to say that the outward expressions of Orthodox worship are always more beautiful than those to be found in the West. That would be to reduce the matter largely to a question of individual taste. And, indeed, ugliness is to be found in Orthodox churches, as it is elsewhere, though perhaps not quite so often; ugliness as blatant as that polished alabaster and those brazen whatnots which make us wince in many a Victorian church.

But the phrase "aesthetic approach" must not be taken in too narrow a sense. The "aesthetic approach" of Orthodoxy is not only *through* beauty but also *in* beauty, and it involves the reception *of* beauty. It is the sense of the beauty of the unseen world, which is reflected in this world, which dominates it. The Orthodox feeling for religion is a vital awareness of the Resurrection of Christ as a source of salving, reinvigorating power which is to rescue and transform the whole Cosmos. Its goal is the rescue of all creation from corruption, the transfiguration of the Cosmos, the restoration of its original beauty, as well as of its pristine goodness. Thus the icon, for instance, is not only a human attempt to achieve beauty and offer it in the service of God. It is much more a scrap of the material world which has been rescued from corruption and made a vehicle by which the unseen world comes into touch with men and in which the divine beauty dwells.

Thus in the flux and confusion of the modern world where men are groping for new certainties amid the ruins of bygone stabilities, Orthodoxy proclaims a definite body of beliefs anchored in historical facts, and expresses that belief in worship. It is, therefore, conscious of a mission to the world. It is aware of its Orthodox life as a cleansing, restoring and transfiguring agency in a world which "lies in evil".

It may with justice be said that for long periods that sense of mission has lain dormant. Or at least that owing largely to the political environment in which the Orthodox Church was set and to which its hierarchy has too often been submissive, the sense of mission has failed to find active expression. But it was never dead, and from time to time it awakes and demands new outlets and new methods of presenting Orthodoxy to the world as new circumstances arise and the conscience of the Church is quickened to meet them.

A notable example is the Zoe Movement in Greece which was founded in 1907 and came into public notice with the appearance of its periodical *Zoe* a few years later. The move-

ment originated in a brotherhood, the members of which took
no permanent vows and had no rigid rule. But they lived in
common; the majority of them were laymen, and they were
trained theologians. They were an unofficial independent
body and as such had to meet some opposition at first. Their
purpose was first to live the Orthodox life themselves, and
then to bring it home to the masses of the people in Greece.
The members of the Zoe Brotherhood were teachers, they
fostered the revival of preaching and set up a press for the
printing of cheap books of religious instruction and devotion.
(Not so very long before this, according to the former Archbishop of Corinth, nine-tenths of the Greek parochial clergy
were incapable of writing their own names.)[1] They laid great
stress upon Confession, and they organized Sunday schools.
Their efforts met with much success and the response of the
people was visible and striking.

A rather different illustration of the recuperative strength
of Orthodoxy is afforded by the action of the Russian Church
in the period between the two revolutions of 1917. In August
and September of that year, in spite of the condition of civil
disorder, the Council of the Russian Church met in Moscow
and set itself vigorously to the task of reform. The former
Holy Synod abolished itself, and the Patriarchate was restored.
The Church turned to the reorganization of its own government in view of the changes which had taken place in civic life.
An extensive programme of work was undertaken by the Council
in its 170 sittings, and the fact that much of it was rendered
ineffective by subsequent developments in the relations of
Church and State should not be allowed to disguise the inherent
vigour and the faith in Orthodoxy which the Council revealed.[1]

The remarkable cohesive strength in the Orthodox Communion is a fact to be noted. Since the time of the breakaway
of the Monophysites described in Chapter II, the Orthodox
world has remained one united family of Churches, in spite
of temporary estrangements and quarrels. They are held
together by no monarchical system of government, but,

[1] See *The Christian East*, July, 1937, and December, 1937.
[1] See an account of this period by a Russian writer in the Sixth Report
of *The Anglican and Eastern Churches Association*, 1921.

according to their own account, by community of faith and
love. In this respect their life is in striking contrast with the
fissiparous tendencies displayed by the West. The Orthodox
Church includes men of different races and languages, they
are frankly national in outlook, they worship in the language
of the people, not in a common and liturgical tongue. There
are marked divergencies of temperament, especially between
Greek and Slav which run like an undercurrent beneath the
surface of their history and threaten disruption, as much now
as ever. Yet in spite of all this the Orthodox Communion
holds together and retains its identity. The case of Bulgaria
serves but to underline the fact. For the schism which occurred
in 1871 between Constantinople and the Bulgarian Church,
precisely on the grounds of what the former regarded as the
excessive nationalism of the latter, has now at length been
healed, and Bulgaria is once more restored to the full communion of Orthodoxy. This unity in diversity which maintains
itself in the face of so many factors which might make for
disintegration, and which owes its existence to no coercive
principle but to bonds which are intangible and belong to the
moral and spiritual sphere, is an impressive fact of which a
disordered world may well take note.

If the life of the Orthodox Church in past centuries has
been conspicuously defensive, a rôle of guardianship of its
faith and a willingness to suffer in its defence, the twentieth
century has revealed the fact that such a life has not ceased to
be the vocation of Orthodoxy. The geographical situation of
the Orthodox peoples in Eastern Europe places them in a
peculiarly exposed position in the conflict which atheistic
Communism wages with all forms of religion. This conflict
is something new in the modern world. The Christian creed
and way of life have been rejected before by individual people
or small groups. Alternative creeds have been proposed and
accepted, more or less in the seclusion of the study. But the
twentieth century has seen the proclamation of rival creeds to
the Christian in the market place, publicly, with explicit
claims to be superior, supported by argument and backed
perhaps by force. Communism, with its definite philosophy of
history and its altruistic appeal on behalf of the downtrodden

and oppressed, has made vast numbers of converts at the expense of Christianity.

This is not the place to discuss the compatibility of Communism with Christianity in theory. It has claims to be regarded as in itself a religion, inasmuch as it has its own philosophy of life which is totalitarian in character, and an equipment of fundamental ideas which claims the allegiance of the whole personality and seeks to control every aspect of life. It insists upon rigid and impeccable orthodoxy in its party members; it has its heresy hunts in the form of purges, its sacred texts and its official interpretation of them. Like Christianity itself, it has its Golden Age in the future, not in the past, but for the Communist the Golden Age will be reached within the confines of this world and within historical time.

Communism has secured political power in the countries of Eastern Europe and here it finds itself face to face with Orthodoxy. If in Yugoslavia the interesting fact has come to light that politically Communism can assume a form which deviates in some respects from the Soviet pattern, yet its attitude to religion remains that of Communism elsewhere when in power. The crux of the conflict lies in the fact that Christianity also claims the whole man, body, soul and spirit, and neither can in theory tolerate the existence of another *total* allegiance. The clash is emphasized by the fact that Communism regards this other allegiance as an aberration of the human mind, and the idea of the spiritual principle in man as an illusion.

So far as words are concerned freedom of religion is guaranteed under Communist rule, but the Communist has his own meaning for the word freedom, as he has for many other words, and in practice Orthodoxy, in common with other forms of religion, faces attack.

It is subject on the one hand to a stream of propaganda of which perhaps the most potent aspect is the explicit assumption that religion is due simply to lack of education. On the other hand it suffers from insidious attempts to undermine the position of religious leaders and to discredit them in public opinion. This may culminate in a trial, the pattern of which has become familiar and may include the uncanny and macabre "confession" of the accused.

Meanwhile, pending the disappearance of religion unde the influence of enlightened education, Communism is pr pared to use it as a tool. Like art, literature, history and scienc religion also is to be pressed or cajoled whenever possible in the service of the Communist *Weltanschauung*. The case Bulgaria may suffice as an instance. In June, 1948, a letter w sent from the Department for Religious Affairs in the Bu garian Foreign Ministry to the Holy Synod of the Bulgaria Orthodox Church, the head of which, the Exarch Stepan, wit the Synod behind him, had attracted the attention of th Government by his wise but firm attitude in defence of th rights of the Church and the claims of religion. The lett contained the following sentences :

"The representatives of the Church must not criticiz the people's rising of 9th September, 1944, and the subse quent change of government."

"The nationalization of private industry and the mine must have the approval and daily support of the hierarch of the Church."

"The representatives of the Church must stress, i their daily work, their respect for the State and the acknowledgment that the State stands above the Churcl and that the Church fulfils the laws of the People's Republi and the State's discipline."

"It is further required that the Church should mak certain changes in the educational system of her institute where—the government claims—subjects are taught whicl contradict the scientific knowledge of the evolution of natur and society and which are opposed to the democratic an progressive spirit."

"It is desirable that the Church use the pulpit, th Church press and private talks for the education of th faithful in love for the state leaders of Bulgaria and Sovie Russia and to ask that their portraits be placed in publi places and private homes."

There was, moreover, a significant note that the reply t this letter should be signed individually by each member o the Synod.

The solid front of the Synod disintegrated under pressure
brought to bear upon its individual members, and Stepan
found himself obliged to resign.

The general picture must not be drawn too much in
sheer black and white. There is a Communism which is not
the sworn foe of religion; and even when it is, it is well to recall
Berdyaev's frequent warning that even the fight against God
may be a form of affirming God if it is a protest against un-
worthy conceptions of God which have allowed cruelty and
injustice to prevail in human life.[1]

But so far as the Orthodox Church in the Communist
State is concerned, we may remember that Orthodoxy has
tried conclusions with the secular power before. In the interests
of political unity the Byzantine Emperors often tried to force
it to come to terms with heresy, as later they endeavoured to
impose upon it union with Rome upon Rome's conditions in
order to save the State. There was everything to be said for
the Emperor's attitude from the worldly point of view and
much perhaps from the spiritual point of view also. But
Orthodoxy refused to compromise. Henri Grégoire assures us
that it is no paradox to represent the religious history of
Byzantium as a conflict between the Church and the State,
from which the Church emerged unquestionably the victor.[2]

Orthodoxy lived for centuries under the harsh Government
of the Turk. But with the coming of political emancipation, it
is found to have retained its faith intact, its identity unimpaired
and its unity preserved. It has known how to bend before the
storm and, unbroken, to abide its time. Doubtless it has had
its sinners, its time-servers even in high places. But the two-
fold cry of Orthodoxy "Lord have mercy" and "Glory be to
Thee O Lord", has rung out above them all, and still rings
out. The host of its saints and prelates and of common folk
held fast to their faith in the power of the Resurrection to
transform the whole world, and they have seen and see in
Orthodoxy the authentic faith of Christ, for which many of
them have been prepared to die.

[1] See the Report of the Lambeth Conference, 1948, Part II, p. 20 ff.,
London, 1948.
[2] Baynes and Moss : *Byzantium*, p. 130.

BIBLIOGRAPHY

This is a brief list of books and is limited to those written in or translated into English.

Those who are approaching the subject for the first time may be advised to read some of the following :

F. G. Cole: *The Mother of All Churches*, London, 1908.
M. Constantinides: *The Orthodox Church*, London, 1931.
R. M. French: *Serbian Church Life*, London, 1942.
C. Zvegintzov: *Our Mother Church*, London, 1948 (designed specially for the instruction of children among the Russian exiles).
M. Zernov: *The Church of the Eastern Christians*, London, 1942.

For further study of the subject in general there are:

A. K. Fortescue: *The Orthodox Eastern Church*, London, 1927. Full of information, which is all presented from the Roman Catholic point of view).
W. F. Adeney: *The Greek and Eastern Churches*, Edinburgh, 1908.
B. J. Kidd: *The Churches of Eastern Christendom*, London, 1927.
J. M. Neale: *A History of the Holy Eastern Church*, Part I. General Introduction. 2 Vols. London, 1850.
S. Bulgakov: *The Orthodox Church*, London, 1935.

For the earlier period:

N. H. Baynes: *The Byzantine Empire*, London, 1926.
N. H. Baynes and H. St. L. B. Moss (Ed.), *Byzantium*, Oxford, 1948.
H. St. L. B. Moss: *The Birth of the Middle Ages*, Oxford, 1935.
M. Spinka: *Christianity in the Balkans*, Chicago, 1933. (Down to the Turkish Conquest).
F. Dvornik: *The Photian Schism*, Camb., 1948.
W. A. Wigram: *The Separation of the Monophysites*, London, 1923.
G. Every: *The Byzantine Patriarchate*, London, 1947.

On the Patriarchate of Jerusalem:

A. Bertram and J. W. A. Young. Report of the Commission

appointed by the Government of Palestine to inquire and report upon certain controversies between the Orthodox Patriarchate of Jerusalem and the Arab Orthodox Community. Oxford, 1926.

T. E. DOWLING: *The Orthodox Greek Patriarchate of Jerusalem*, London, 1913.

On Russia:

P. ANDERSON: *People, Church and State in Modern Russia*, London, 1944.

N. BERDYAEV: *The Origin of Russian Communism*, London, 1936.

G. P. FEDOTOV: *The Russian Religious Mind*, Harvard, 1946.

G. P. FEDOTOV: *A Treasury of Russian Spirituality*, London, 1950.

G. P. FEDOTOV: *The Russian Church since the Revolution*, London, 1928.

W. H. FRERE: *Links in the Chain of Russian Church History*, London, 1918.

N. GORODETZKY: *The Humiliated Christ in Modern Russian Thought*, London, 1938.

A. N. MOURAVIEFF: *A History of the Church of Russia* (down to 1721), English Translation by Blackmore. London, 1842.

N. ZERNOV: *The Russians and Their Church*, London, 1945.

G. B. H. BISHOP: *The Religion of Russia*, London, 1915.

L. E. RIDDING: *The Travels of Macarius*, London, 1936.

On Orthodox Monasticism:

H. DELEHAYE: Chapter V in *Byzantium* (Baynes & Moss).

F. W. HASLUCK: *Athos and its Monasteries*, London, 1924.

N. F. ROBINSON: *Monasticism in the Orthodox Churches*, London, 1916 (technical).

R. M. DAWKINS: *The Monks of Athos*, London, 1936.

On Orthodox Doctrine:

Of the Symbolic Books mentioned in Chapter VI, Mogila's Catechism and the Confessions of Dositheus have been translated into English. The former is:

J. J. OVERBECK: *The Orthodox Confession of Peter Mogila*, London, 1898.

The latter is to be found in :

J. N. W. B. ROBERTSON: *The Synod of Jerusalem*, London, 1899, and also in:

G. WILLIAMS: *The Orthodox and the Non-Jurors*, London, 1868.

W. E. DANIEL (trans.): *The Holy Catechism of Nicolas Bulgaris*, London, 1893.

R. W. BLACKMORE: *The Doctrine of the Russian Church*, Aberdeen, 1845 (contains Philaret's Longer Catechism).
F. GAVIN: *Some Aspects of Contemporary Greek Orthodox Thought*, London, 1936.
A. C. HEADLAM: *The Teaching of the Russian Church*, London, 1897.

Translations of Liturgical Texts:
The Orthodox Liturgy, London, S.P.C.K., 1939.
I. F. HAPGOOD: *Service Book of the Holy Orthodox Catholic Apostolic Church*, New York, 1922.
A. RILEY: *Guide to the Divine Liturgy in the East*, London, 1922.
See also:
ANON: *A Manual of Eastern Orthodox Prayers*, London, 1945.
ANON: *Orthodox Spirituality*, London, 1945.
N. GOGOL: *Meditations on the Divine Liturgy*, London, 1926.
    A series of small books giving the Greek and English Texts of the chief Orthodox Services on opposite pages, is published by Williams & Norgate (various dates between 1914 and 1948). The Liturgy of St. John Chrysostom in the same series is published by the Faith Press (1930).

On Relations with the Anglican Church:
J. A. DOUGLAS: *Relations of the Anglican Churches with the Eastern Orthodox*, London, 1921.
W. J. BIRBECK: *Russia and the English Church*, London, 1895.
A. RILEY: *Birkbeck and the Russian Church*, London, 1917.
C. ANDROUTSOS: *The Validity of English Ordinations*, London, 1909.
G. WILLIAMS: *The Orthodox and the Non-Jurors*, London, 1868.
See also:
Eirene (A Periodical published by the Anglican and Eastern Churches Union between 1908 and 1914).
The Christian East (The Quarterly Magazine of the Anglican and Eastern Churches Association from 1920 to 1938. New series, 1950). And the *Reports* of the same Society (present address: 63, Ladbroke Grove, W.11).
Sobornost (Journal of the Fellowship of St. Alban and St. Sergius, 52, Ladbroke Grove, W.11).
There is a Roman Catholic Review called *The Eastern Churches Quarterly* (St. Augustine's Abbey, Ramsgate).

On Life and Religion:
N. BAYNES and E. DAWES: *Three Byzantine Saints*, Oxford, 1948.
M. CONSTANTINIDES: *Life and work in the Diocese of Athens*, London, no date.
        M

R. M. FRENCH: *The Way of a Pilgrim*, London, 1930 and 1941; *The Pilgrim continues his Way*, London, 1943 (translated from the Russian).

S. GRAHAM: *The Way of Martha and the Way of Mary*, London, 1914.

S. GRAHAM: *With the Russian Pilgrims to Jerusalem*, London, 1914.

The Life of the Archpriest Avvakum by Himself, London, 1924.

On Art:

N. P. KONDAKOV: *The Russian Icon*, has been translated into English (by E. H. Muins, Oxford, 1927), but is not always easily available. Smaller books are:

D. TALBOT RICE: *Russian Ikons*, London, 1947.

T. TALBOT RICE: *Russian Art*, London, 1949.

G. MATHEW: *Byzantine Painting*, London, 1950.

M. BEGA: *Byzantine Art in Rumania*. London, 1940.

D. R. BUXTON: *Russian Mediaeval Architecture*, Cambridge, 1934.

INDEX